mini quilting

QUICK-TO-SEW DESIGNS TO USE UP FABRIC FROM YOUR STASH

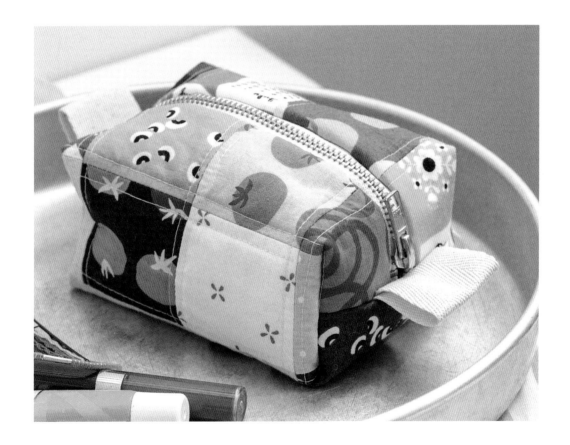

laura strutt

CICO BOOKS

LONDON NEW YORK

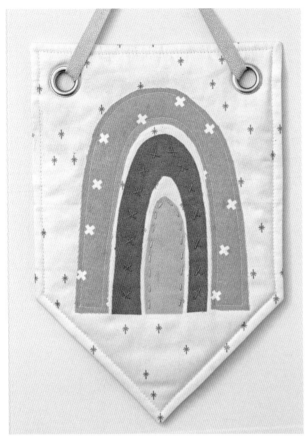

For Ethan Wolf and Elkie Raven—
no matter what

Published in 2025 by CICO Books
An imprint of Ryland Peters & Small Ltd
20–21 Jockey's Fields, London WC1R 4BW
1452 Davis Bugg Road, Warrenton, NC 27589

www.rylandpeters.com

10 9 8 7 6 5 4 3 2 1

Text © Laura Strutt 2025
Design, illustration, and photography
© CICO Books 2025

A CIP catalog record for this book is available from
the Library of Congress and the British Library.

ISBN: 978 1 80065 407 5

Printed in China

Designer: Alison Fenton
Photographer: James Gardiner
Stylist: Nel Haynes
Illustrator: Cathy Brear
Artworks on pages 119 (left and top and bottom
right), 120–122, 123 (top), 124: Stephen Dew
Binding artworks on page 123: Carrie Hill
Templates: Stephen Dew
The techniques on page 120 are from *Quilting Basics*
by Michael Caputo.

In-house editor: Jenny Dye
Art director: Sally Powell
Creative director: Leslie Harrington
Production manager: Gordana Simakovic
Publishing manager: Carmel Edmonds

contents

chapter 1

extra-mini makes 8

chapter 2

bags & pouches 48

chapter 3

home & wall décor 72

introduction

I can recall the first ever patchwork piece I created—at age 6 in the Brownies (the UK equivalent of the Girl Scouts), working each week to hand-sew a new folded layer of fabric in place to create a Folded Star or Somerset Patchwork. Since then, quilting has become a beloved hobby of mine for many reasons. The process of selecting fabrics, piecing them together, and creating intricate designs is both meditative and rewarding. The final product, a cozy and unique quilted piece, holds sentimental value and can be passed down through generations. The art of quilting allows for self-expression and creativity, making it a truly cherished craft.

Over the years I have loved seeing galleries of bold and arresting modern quilting designs and am equally charmed and inspired by antique and traditional quilts. Quilting is a craft that combines creativity, precision, and a touch of nostalgia. For many quilters, the joy of quilting extends beyond the finished product to the process itself. One of the most rewarding ways to quilt is by using scrap fabrics to create mini quilting projects. It allows you to use up leftover materials, try out new techniques, and create something beautiful and unique.

These projects not only help reduce waste but also offer an opportunity to experiment with new techniques and designs on a smaller, more manageable scale. Mini quilts are perfect for quilters of all levels. They are quick to make, require fewer materials, and allow for a great deal of creativity. Whether you're a beginner looking to practice your skills or an experienced quilter wanting to try out new patterns, mini quilts and mini quilting projects are an ideal canvas.

Whether you hang your finished pieces on your walls or give them as gifts, mini quilts are a testament to the creativity and resourcefulness of you, the quilter. So gather your scraps, unleash your creativity, and start your next mini quilting adventure!

before you begin

If you're new to quilting or you need to refresh your memory, check out the techniques section on page 119.

All seam allowances are sewn with a straight machine stitch. The standard seam allowance for the projects in this book is ¼in (0.5cm), unless the project instructions tell you otherwise. Do a couple of reverse stitches at the start and finish of each seam to lock the stitches.

Each of the projects has a skill rating, from 1 to 3, indicated by the colored bars at the side of each project title. Start with the level 1 projects then move on to the next two levels as you build your skills and confidence.

materials

fabrics

Fabrics are the heart of any quilting project. As quilts are traditionally made using small amounts of fabrics or scraps, they are a great way to repurpose materials or use what you already have in your stash. The majority of the projects here are made using cotton. If you work with a different fabric, be sure to use the same fiber throughout a project to help give it a neat finish.

While you will need to use larger pieces of fabric for the backing and binding fabrics, the majority of these projects can be made from offcuts, scraps, or even pre-cut bundles.

There are several different pre-cut fabric sizes available for quilting, each with their own unique measurements. Some common options include Charm Packs, Jelly Rolls, Layer Cakes, and Fat Quarters. These pre-cut fabrics are convenient as they are often in a color- or style-themed bundle, and are cut to a precise size ready to use.

Common pre-cut fabric sizes are:
Mini Charm Pack: 2½in (6cm) square
Charm Pack: 5in (12.5cm) square
Layer Cakes: 10in (25cm) squares
Jelly Roll or Strip Roll: 2½ x 44in (6.5 x 112cm) strips
Fat Quarter: 18 x 22in (50 x 56cm)
Thin Quarter: 9 x 44in (25 x 112cm)
Fat Eighth: 9 x 22in (25 x 56cm)

Tips for using scrap fabrics

The first step in creating mini quilted projects is gathering the scrap fabrics. These might be leftovers from previous projects, fabric swatches, or even old clothing. The beauty of using scraps is that they come in a variety of different colors and patterns which will add interest and a splash of your personality to your make.

Sort by color and size
Organize your scraps by color and size. This will make it easier to plan which fabrics are suitable for which projects. Making a note of the dimensions of the fabrics and pinning it to the top is a great way to stay organized with a large stash!

Mix and match
Don't be afraid to mix different prints or solids. The eclectic look is part of the charm of a scrap quilt.

Mood board
If you have favorite color comminations, keep small scraps and pin them together to build a style mood board that will help you when working a fabric selection for future projects.

Get balance
Busy prints and bold colors can sometimes be hard to coordinate with other scraps. Try arranging the fabrics for your project and take a photo using a digital or phone camera. Using the grayscale option to edit the photo allows you to see the selection in terms of the balance and tonal ranges. This can help you to create visually cohesive and balanced selections of scrap fabrics.

FABRIC TERMS

Low volume fabrics
These are neutral, cream, white or pale-colored print fabrics with a subtle design. They are used to offset bold colors and busy prints and provide balance in your finished design.

Directional prints
These are prints that have a design that can only be used one way up. Non-directional prints (such as polka dots or geometric designs) can be used any way up.

Batting (wadding)

Quilt batting, also known as wadding, is the layer of material that is placed between the quilt top and the backing fabric. It adds insulation, warmth, and structure to the quilt. Several different types are available, and the choice of batting depends on various factors, including warmth, breathability, sustainability, and durability.

Wool batting is renowned for its exceptional warmth, making it an excellent choice for bed quilts or winter projects.

Cotton and bamboo batting offer superior breathability, allowing for temperature regulation. These options are often used for projects made for babies and children.

Bamboo batting is not only breathable but also considered a more sustainable option.

Polyester batting is both durable and easy to launder and is a great choice for home décor items and wall hangings.

Interlining (interfacing)

Alongside batting, interlining (also known as interfacing) is used in quilting projects to add structure or as a foundation for the work. Some of the projects in this book include iron-on interlinings and fusible foam. These can be found in craft or sewing stores.

thread

Quilters often select threads based on not only on the color but also the weight and style of the thread. The larger the wt (weight) number, the finer the thread. Many quilters prefer to work with all-cotton threads, and a 50wt/2-ply cotton thread is ideal for piecing (sewing pieces of fabric together). When machine-quilting lines onto a piece, you can work with the same 50wt cotton or you can use a heavier weight thread, for example 40wt or 28wt, to create more dominant quilting designs. You can also select thread colors that complement or contrast with the fabric to enhance the look of the quilt.

basic quilting kit

As well as a sewing machine, quilting requires a few additional tools that will help to make the process of cutting, preparing, and sewing your projects easier and more successful.

Sewing machine

The majority of the projects in this book were created using a sewing machine. I used the Janome DSK100 and the Janome Memory Craft 9480 QC Professional. The main requirements you will need from your machine are to sew a straight machine stitch that has an adjustable length. Some of the projects in this book require a zipper foot to sew in zippers. A walking foot is also useful, as it prevents multiple layers of fabric from slipping when you are sewing them. You can also drop the feed dogs on your machine and use a free-motion foot to create free-motion quilting designs. A quilting guide bar (see page 123) is also useful for quilting straight lines.

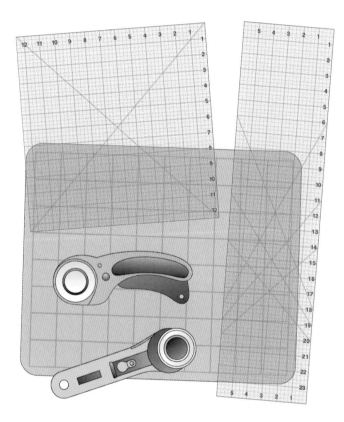

Rotary cutter, quilting ruler, and self-healing mat

Quilting requires lots of cutting and trimming. In many cases the pieces need to be trimmed to an exact size. Using a rotary cutter and quilting ruler to cut the pieces on a self-healing mat is ideal as they allow you to cut neat, even pieces every time.

USING A ROTARY CUTTER

■ Pay close attention to the blade when picking up your rotary cutter, as it is extremely sharp.

■ Be sure to use the cover when your rotary cutter is not in use.

■ Always cut away from your body.

Fabric scissors (large and small)

Use scissors with blades that are 7–8in (18–20cm) long for general cutting such as circles or appliqué shapes. Small scissors are ideal for trimming and clipping seams and cutting loose threads. Never use your fabric scissors to cut paper, as this will blunt the blades.

Seam ripper

This tool is used for unpicking incorrect stitches and seams. The sharp point glides under the stitch while the blade breaks the thread. Always keep the cover on your seam ripper when it's not in use.

Iron, pressing mat, and pressing cloth

Pressing is one of the key steps in any sewing project and this is also true for quilting. A domestic iron and ironing board will work great for these projects, especially when you are preparing backing fabrics or pressing pieces prior to cutting.

A small wool-felt pressing mat and a mini iron are also great additions to your quilting kit. The smaller plate of a mini iron makes it easy to handle, which is helpful when pressing small areas. Mini irons often heat up very fast, making them more convenient than larger irons when pressing elements throughout the process of making a project.

A wool-felt pressing mat not only provides a smooth and even surface for pressing fabric, but also helps to retain heat, allowing for more effective pressing. The dense and firm nature of the wool felt helps to prevent any distortion and stretching of the fabric, which will aid the construction of your quilt projects.

A pressing cloth—either a piece of white cotton to avoid dye transfer, or a store-bought one such as a Vlieseline Iron On Cloth—is essential for protecting delicate fabrics from heat damage and preventing shiny marks or imprints. It is lightly dampened and placed on top of your fabric before pressing. It acts as a barrier between the iron and the fabric, allowing for even heat distribution and preventing direct contact. A pressing cloth can also help to prevent the iron plate from coming into contact with any adhesives when using fusible interlinings or battings (waddings).

Seam roller

This handy tool is great for pressing seams and small sections, as an alternative to finger-pressing. The roller section is used to apply even pressure to small areas of fabric and is great for English Paper Piecing and Foundation Paper Piecing projects.

Pins and clips

Quilting requires lots of layers or pieces of fabric to be held together at a time, and pins and clips will help you to hold these elements in exactly the right position.

Long, flat-headed pins are great for holding fabrics in place ready for sewing and, due to the length of the pin, they can help with aligning seams.

Fabric clips are fantastic for holding sections together during all stages of the constructions process and are ideal for fabrics that you don't want to damage, for example clear vinyl.

Quilting safety pins are great for pin-basting a project before you quilt it. They have a curved shaft, allowing you to ease them through all the layers of a quilt to hold the pieces securely in place ahead of the quilting process.

Markers

There are lots of instances when you will need to mark your quilt project, for example to add a stitching guide, a quilting motif, or to aid the construction. There are a wide range of markers available, from chalk to water- and heat-erasable markers. Always be sure to test the marker on a scrap of your fabric, to be certain you can remove it without leaving a trace on the finished piece.

You can also use a creasing tool, also known as a Hera marker (shown on the right). Use this tool either free-hand or in combination with a ruler, and apply pressure to create distinct creases on the the surface of the fabrics. The creases can be easily removed by ironing or washing.

chapter 1
extra-mini makes

lanyard and key fob

Whether you use it for holding a work pass or an entry ticket to a quilt expo, this colorful lanyard will help you stand out from the crowd. Plus, you can use the same method to create a matching key fob with a handy loop that makes it easy to find in your bag or purse.

FABRIC AND MATERIALS

Cotton fabric scraps in a selection of prints, each minimum size 3 x 18in (7.5 x 46cm)

Medium-weight non-woven fusible interlining, Vlieseline H250, 3 x 46in (7.5 x 117cm)

Coordinating thread

KAM snap or snap fastening, ½in (1.2cm) wide

Lanyard hardware, 1³⁄₁₆in (3cm) wide

Key fob hardware, 1in (2.5cm) wide

TOOLS AND EQUIPMENT

Basic quilting kit (see page 6)

KAM snap tool

Pliers for affixing key fob hardware

Tailor's awl (optional, see tips)

FINISHED MEASUREMENTS

Lanyard: 1in (2.5cm) wide x 17in (43cm) long (excluding hardware)

Key fob: 1in (2.5cm) wide x 5in (12.5cm) long (excluding hardware)

CUTTING INSTRUCTIONS

Print cotton fabric scraps: Cut a selection of strips, each 2½in (6.5cm) wide x 1½–3in (4–7.5cm) long

Medium-weight non-woven fusible interlining: Cut one strip measuring 1 x 17½in (2.5 x 44.5cm), and one strip measuring 1 x 18¼in (2.5 x 46.5cm), for the lanyard. Cut one strip measuring 1 x 10¼in (2.5 x 26cm), for the key fob.

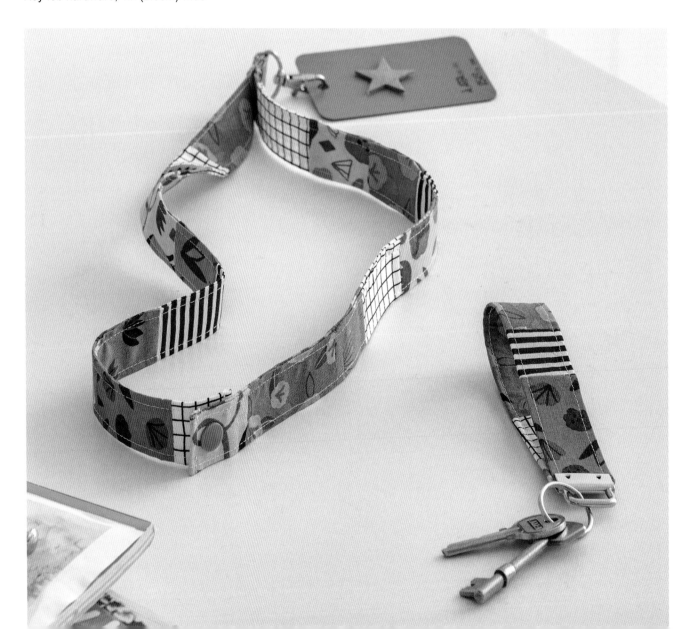

lanyard

1 Select a range of scraps and lay them out with the right sides uppermost to create two strips, one measuring 20in (51cm) and the other 22in (56cm). Arrange the fabrics until you are happy with the placement.

2 Begin joining the pieces of the 20in (51cm) strip together. Working from left to right, place the first two pieces together with right sides facing. Align the raw edges, pin or clip in place, and sew together (see page 121). Press the seam neatly open (see page 119). Continue joining each square in turn. Join the second strip in the same manner.

3 Using the rotary cutter, trim the shorter strip to measure 17¾in (45cm) and the longer strip to measure 18½in (47cm). Place the 17½in (44.5cm) interlining strip on the shorter strip so the adhesive side is facing the wrong side of the fabric. Position the interlining strip ¼in (0.5cm) away from one long raw edge and ¼in (0.5cm) away from each short raw edge. Cover with a pressing cloth and iron to fuse in place. Repeat for the longer lanyard strip and piece of interlining.

TIPS

Bag hardware, such as lanyard swivel clips and key fob attachments, can often be found in craft stores or from specialist bag-making suppliers. You can buy a range of tools to apply the hardware, but you may find that standard pliers will work just as well. If you are using standard pliers, place a piece of batting between the pliers and the hardware—this will prevent any scratches on the the metal.

When working with layers of interfaced fabric, like on this lanyard, work the stitches slowly and carefully. You can use the point of a tailor's awl to help keep the layers in place as you work them through the machine, without risking having your fingertips too close to the needle.

4 Fold each long side of one of the strips to the wrong side by ¼in (0.5cm) and press. Fold the strip in half so that the two long sides meet and press. The raw edges are now concealed inside the folded strip. Pin or clip in place.
Increase the sewing machine stitch length to 3. Taking a ⅛in (3mm) seam allowance from the edges, topstitch (see page 119) along each long side. Zigzag stitch across each short end to neaten. Repeat this step for the second strip.

5 Place the two strips on top of each other, aligning the long edges, with the long strip underneath and extending 1½in (4cm) beyond the end of the short strip. Place the lanyard hardware onto the extended section of the long strip.

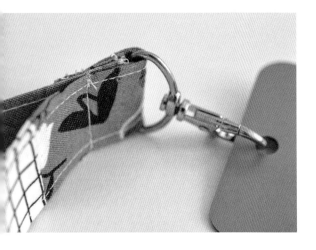

6 Fold the extended section over to cover both the hardware and the raw edge of the second strip and pin or clip in place. Increase the stitch length to 3. Sew to join the two pieces—this will keep the lanyard hardware in place.

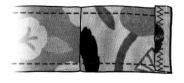

7 Check that the two strips of the lanyard aren't twisted. On the two free short ends, fold the zigzag-stitched edges to the wrong sides by ¼in (0.5cm) and pin or clip in place. Sew along each fold to secure it.

8 Following the manufacturer's instructions, secure a KAM snap or a snap fastening to each end of the lanyard, close to the folded-over section, to finish.

Finishing

Trim any excess threads on the Lanyard and Key Fob, and press lightly to neaten.

key fob

1 Follow step 1 of the Lanyard to lay out a selection of print-cotton strips with the right sides uppermost to create a strip measuring 12in (30cm). Arrange the fabrics until you are happy with the placement.

2 Follow step 2 of the Lanyard to join the pieces together. Using the rotary cutter, ruler, and cutting mat, trim the strip to measure 10½in (26.5cm).

3 Follow step 3 the Lanyard to fuse the interlining strip to the wrong side of the fabric.

4 Follow step 4 of the Lanyard to fold and topstitch the fabric strip and zigzag stitch across each short end.

5 Fold the key fob strip in half and align the two short edges. Place the short edges inside the key fob hardware and secure in place using the pliers. Follow the finishing instructions above.

bookmark

This bookmark is great for using up fabric offcuts and scraps. It is worked by placing the fabrics directly onto a piece of batting and sewing each one in place in turn before pressing open to reveal the finished design.

FABRIC AND MATERIALS

Fabric scraps in a selection of prints

Batting (wadding), 3 x 8in (7.5 x 20cm)

Cotton twill tape ribbon, ⅜in (1cm) wide and 4in (10cm) long

Coordinating thread

TOOLS AND EQUIPMENT

Basic quilting kit (see page 6)

FINISHED MEASUREMENTS

2½in x 7in (6.5 x 17.8cm), excluding twill loop

CUTTING INSTRUCTIONS

Print cotton fabric scraps: Cut a selection of strips, each 3 x 4in (7.5 x 10cm)

1 Select your first two scraps of fabric. Position one scrap onto one side of the batting strip. The right side of the scrap should be facing up.

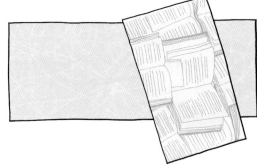

2 Place the second fabric scrap on top, so the right sides of the fabrics are together. Check that once stitched with a seam allowance of ¼in (0.5cm) along the right-hand raw edges and opened out, the second strip will cover the end of the batting. Pin or clip into place. Sew along the right-hand edges to join the two scraps onto the batting.

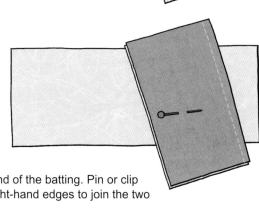

TIP

This design is only lightly quilted. You may prefer to add a few lines of machine- or hand-quilting as desired. If you are making one of these bookmarks as a gift, you could embroider the recipient's name across the length of the bookmark.

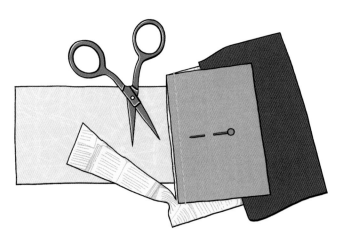

3 Press the fabric, then open the top piece along the seam. Place the next scrap on top of the first piece. You can arrange the fabrics any orientation you like, and you don't have to align the raw edges—just ensure that each new piece will cover the width of the batting below when pressed open. Pin in place. Sew to join the new scrap onto the first piece and the batting. Trim away any excess fabrics from the scrap below to reduce the bulk, being careful not to cut through the stitches or the batting. Open out the third piece along the seam and press.

4 Continue with this method of pinning the fabrics right sides together, sewing in place, and pressing the fabric open. Repeat until the batting is covered in fabric.

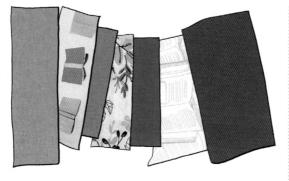

TIP
As you can work with offcuts and scraps, you may like to place the fabrics onto the batting and arrange them before sewing, or you can be more organic in your selection. When placing fabrics, be sure to consider any with directional prints that need to be a certain way up, and ensure that the scraps will cover the width of the batting once stitched and pressed open.

5 Turn the piece over so the batting side is uppermost. Using a rotary cutter, ruler, and cutting mat, trim away the excess fabric along the edges of the batting to neaten. Place the backing fabric onto the back of the batting with the right sides outermost and pin or clip into place.

6 Turn the bookmark over again so the patchwork fabric is uppermost. Sew across the bookmark to add quilting as desired. Here, straight-line machine quilting has been added following the seams in the fabric. Using a rotary cutter, ruler, and cutting mat, trim the bookmark to measure 2½ x 7in (6.5 x 17.8cm). Fold the length of cotton twill tape in half to make a small loop and insert it into the top of the bookmark, positioning it in between the batting and the fabric. Pin or clip in place.

7 Sew around the outer edge of the bookmark, taking a ⅛in (3mm) seam allowance and ensuring the twill tape is secured in the seam. Sew around the edge of the bookmark two more times, close to the first line of stitching.

Finishing
Trim any excess threads and press lightly to neaten.

mug rug

Bigger than a coaster but not as large as a table mat, a mug rug is the perfect size for a cup of coffee or tea and a few of your favorite cookies. This design works with a mini block that is ideal for fussy cutting (see tip) or using offcuts from your stash.

FABRIC AND MATERIALS

Fabric scraps in four different prints: Fabrics A, B, C, and D

Backing fabric, cotton, 7 x 13in (17.8 x 33cm)

Batting (wadding), 7 x 13in (17.8 x 33cm)

Binding, 40in (102cm)

Coordinating thread

TOOLS AND EQUIPMENT

Basic quilting kit (see page 6)

Spray adhesive for basting (optional)

FINISHED MEASUREMENTS

6 x 12in (15 x 30cm)

CUTTING INSTRUCTIONS

FOR THE OHIO STAR

Fabric A: Cut one 2in (5cm) square (fussy cut if desired) for the center block

Fabric B: Cut four 2in (5cm) squares for the corner squares

Fabric C: Cut two 2¾in (7cm) squares for the Quarter Square Triangles (QST)

Fabric D: Cut two 2¾in (7cm) squares for the QST

FOR THE BLOCK BORDER

Fabric B: Cut two 1¼ x 6in (3.2 x 15cm) strips and two 1¼ x 7in (3.2 x 17.8cm) strips

FOR THE SIDE-PANEL STRIPS

Fabric B: Cut one 1½ x 6¼in (4 x 16cm) strip

Fabric C: Cut two 1½ x 6¼in (4 x 16cm) strips

Fabric D: Cut two 1½ x 6¼in (4 x 16cm) strips

TIPS

The Ohio Star block on the mug rug has a fussy-cut motif in its center. Fussy cutting is a method of showcasing a small element of a fabric print. To fussy cut, cut a square of card stock (cardboard) ¼in (0.5cm) larger than the desired square, then using a ruler and craft knife cut the 2in (5cm) square from the center of the card. This leaves a frame at the exact size required for the fussy cut. Move this around the fabric until you get the perfect placement. Use an erasable or water-soluble fabric marker to draw around the inside the aperture. Remove the template and use a rotary cutter and ruler to cut out the fussy-cut square precisely.

This mug rug is created using a small amount of batting. If you are working with offcuts of batting you can join them to create the size you need by placing each straight edge together—butting them up but not overlapping—and working over the join with a large zigzag stitch. Ensure that the stitches are worked over each piece of batting to create ready-to-use "Franken-batting!"

1 Place a Fabric C and Fabric D square right sides together and follow steps 1–4 on page 122 to make two Half Square Triangles (HST), but don't trim away the "dog's ears" in step 5. Press the seam allowance over to the darker fabrics.

2 Layer the two HST together with Fabric C over Fabric D and the right sides facing. The seams should be neatly nested. Draw a line through the center from corner to corner. Sew down each side of the marked line in turn, along the lines marked in pink.

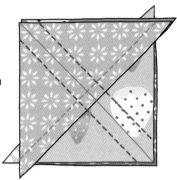

3 Using a rotary cutter, ruler, and mat, cut down the marked line to create two Quarter Square Triangles (QST). Repeat these steps once more to make four QST in total. Open out and press each QST fully and press. Using a rotary cutter, ruler, and mat, trim the excess seam allowances to ensure that each square measures 2in (5cm) square.

4 Arrange the squares into three rows of three squares as follows:

Fabric B (corner), QST, Fabric B (corner)

QST, Fabric A (center), QST

Fabric B (corner), QST, Fabric B (corner)

Ensure that you are happy with the orientation of the fabrics.

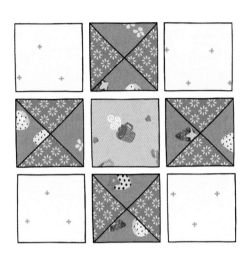

Back of the mug rug

5 Follow steps 1–6 on page 121 to sew the nine-square Ohio Star block together.

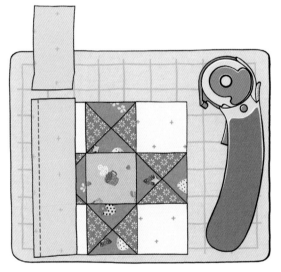

6 Position one of the shorter Fabric B border strips along the left-hand side of the block with the right sides facing. Align the raw edges and pin or clip in place. Sew in place. Using a rotary cutter ruler and mat, trim away the excess border fabric and press neatly open. Repat to sew the second short Fabric B border strip to the right-hand side of the block.

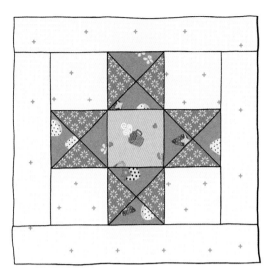

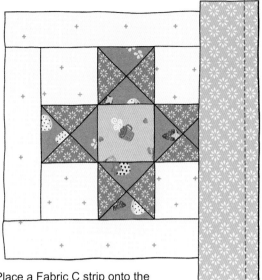

7 Follow step 6 to sew the two long Fabric B border strips to the top and bottom edges of the nine-square block. Press the bordered block fully.

8 Place a Fabric C strip onto the right-hand side of the Ohio Star block and pin or clip in place, aligning the raw edges. Sew the strip in place and press it open.

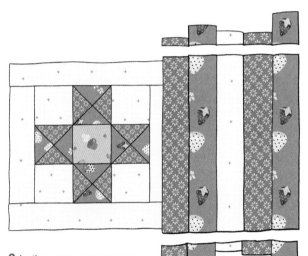

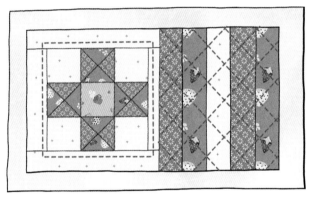

9 In the same manner as step 8, join the remaining strips in the following order: Fabric D, Fabric B, Fabric C, Fabric D. Trim away the excess fabric from the top and bottom of the strips using a rotary cutter, ruler, and mat.

10 Place the backing fabric with the wrong side uppermost. Spray the batting lightly with adhesive on both sides. Place the batting on top of the backing and then place the mug rug panel on top with its right side uppermost. Press lightly to baste the layers together. Quilt the mug rug as desired—here a cross-hatch design has been worked over the strips. Stitch in the ditch (see page 119) has been used to emphasize the Ohio Star block, and straight lines have been sewn around the nine-square block.

11 Using a rotary cutter, ruler, and mat, trim the mug rug to 6 x 12in (15 x 30cm). Follow the steps on page 123 to attach the binding around the edge of the mug rug.

Finishing
Trim any excess threads and press lightly to neaten.

pieced postcards

These patchwork postcards are fun to make and a great way to get creative with your fabric scraps. They can be personalized and make unique gifts for friends and fellow stitchers. These three designs are just a few ideas for getting you started on your own wonderful postcards.

FABRIC AND MATERIALS

Fabric scraps in a selection of prints and solid colors

White cotton backing fabric

Sew-in medium-weight stable pelmet, Vlieseline S80, 4 x 6in (10 x 15cm), for each postcard

Fusible adhesive, Vlieseline Bondaweb, 4 x 6in (10 x 15cm), for each postcard

Coordinating thread

Thin card stock (card), 4 x 6in (10 x 15cm), for each postcard

TOOLS AND EQUIPMENT

Basic quilting kit (see page 6)

Spray adhesive (optional)

Craft glue

FINISHED MEASUREMENTS

4 x 6in (10 x 15cm)

Cutting instructions

FOR EACH POSTCARD:

White cotton backing fabric: Cut one 5 x 7in (12.7 x 17.8cm) piece

APPLIQUÉ POSTCARD:

Background: Cut one 4 x 6in (10 x 15cm) piece

Appliqué motifs (hearts): Cut three small scraps

SCRAPPY STRIPS POSTCARD:

Cotton fabric scraps: Cut a selection of strips, each 1–2in (2.5–5cm) wide and 9in (23cm) long

LOG CABIN POSTCARD:

Cotton fabric scraps:

Accent piece: Cut one 2¾ x 3½in (7 x 9cm) piece

Strip 1: Cut one 1¾ x 3½in (4.5 x 9cm) piece

Strip 2: Cut one 1¼ x 5in (3.2 x 12.7cm) piece

Strip 3: Cut one 1¾ x 4in (4.5 x 10cm) piece

Strip 4: Cut one 1¼ x 6½in (3.2 x 16.5cm) piece

TIPS

These postcards have been created to a standard 4 x 6in (10 x 15cm) size, but you may need to check any restrictions with your postal service or mail carrier before sending to avoid any disappointments.

Bondaweb is a web of iron-on adhesive that has a carrier paper. To remove the paper once fused to the fabric and without damaging the appliqué shapes, gently run the tip of a pin along the surface of the paper. This will score it, allowing you to peel the paper away without damaging the fabric or adhesive webbing below.

appliqué postcard

1 Place the pelmet onto the wrong side of the background fabric and pin, clip, or use spray adhesive to fix it in place as needed.

2 Using an iron and pressing cloth, fuse a piece of Bondaweb onto the wrong side of each of the fabric scraps. Draw your appliqué motifs on the Bondaweb. Here, three hearts have been drawn. Remember that your motifs will be mirrored once cut and placed on the design. Allow the Bondaweb to cool, then cut out the motifs.

3 Tear away the backing papers from each of the motifs (see tip above). Position the motifs onto the front of the postcard, with the adhesive side facing the right side of the background fabric. Cover with a pressing cloth and fuse into place with an iron. Once the fabrics have cooled, work your desired stitching. Here the sewing machine's feed dogs have been dropped to work free-motion stitching. For instructions on making up and finishing, see page 22.

scrappy strips postcard

1 Take two fabric strips and place them together with the right sides facing. Align the raw edges. Pin or clip in place, then sew together.

2 Continue in the same manner, sewing on a new strip each time. Press the seams open (see page 119). Join enough strips to cover the front of the postcard—here the strips are placed on the diagonal and cover the entire surface of the pelmet.

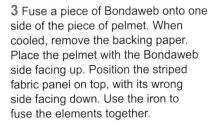

3 Fuse a piece of Bondaweb onto one side of the piece of pelmet. When cooled, remove the backing paper. Place the pelmet with the Bondaweb side facing up. Position the striped fabric panel on top, with its wrong side facing down. Use the iron to fuse the elements together.

4 Using a rotary cutter, ruler and mat, trim the excess fabrics from around the pelmet. Work quilting stitches as desired. For this postcard, straight-line stitching has been sewn to emphasize the diagonal orientation of the strips. For instructions on making up and finishing, see page 22.

log cabin postcard

1 Place the accent fabric with the right side uppermost. Position strip 1 onto the right-hand side of the accent fabric with the right sides facing and the raw edges aligned. Pin or clip and then sew in place.

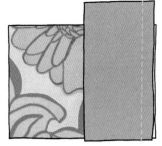

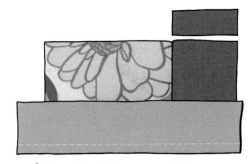

2 Press the fabric open and trim any excess fabric from the strip. Position strip 2 onto the lower side of the accent fabric with the right sides facing. Pin or clip and then sew in place.

3 Press the fabric open and trim any excess fabric from the strip. Working in the same manner, pin and stitch the strip 3 to the left-hand side of the fabric. Press open and trim the excess before adding strip 4 along the top and stitching to secure in the same manner.

4 Fuse a piece of Bondaweb onto one side of the pelmet and when cooled remove the backing paper. Place the pelmet with the Bondaweb side facing up. Position the log cabin panel, with its wrong side facing down, on the pelmet. Use the iron to fuse the elements together. Once the fabrics have cooled, work your desired stitching. Here straight-line quilting has been worked around the center fabric following the log cabin motif.

Making up and finishing

Add the backing by fusing a piece of Bondaweb to the pelmet on the back of the postcard. When cooled, peel away the backing paper. Place the adhesive side onto the backing fabric, cover with a pressing cloth, and fuse into place.

Once cooled trim to 4 x 6in (10 x 15cm) and work around the edges using a zigzag stitch. Modify the stitch settings to ensure the stitches are wide and close set (see tip). To get a dense fill of stitches you can work around the edge of the postcard twice.

Trim any excess threads and press lightly to neaten. Use a thin layer of craft glue to attach the card stock to the wrong side of the postcard. Allow to fully dry before adding a hand-written note and a stamp.

TIP
When making changes to the zigzag stitch, remember the stitch width is the left-to-right measurement of the zigzag stitch and the stitch length is the space between each stitch. For these postcards I used a stitch width of 3 and a stitch length of 0.5–1.

japanese-style folded fabric tub

Create a soft but stable fabric tub using foam interlining. This pretty fabric pot uses a variation of Japanese folded patchwork to work circles of fabric into square blocks, here highlighting the bold statement print.

FABRIC AND MATERIALS

Cotton fabric scraps in a selection of prints, or a fat quarter

Cotton backing fabric

Fusible woven interlining, Vlieseline G700, 25½ x 17in (65 x 43.5cm)

Fusible foam interlining, Style-Vil Fix, 13½ x 9in (34.5 x 23cm)

Coordinating thread

TOOLS AND EQUIPMENT

Basic quilting kit (see page 6)

Compass

Hera marker or knitting needle

Hand-sewing needle

TEMPLATE

Circle—use a compass set to 3½in (8.9cm) to draw a circle with a 7in (17.8cm) diameter and cut it out.

FINISHED MEASUREMENTS

4½in (11.5cm) tall, 4½in (11.5cm) wide, 4½in (11.5cm) deep

CUTTING INSTRUCTIONS

Print cotton fabric scraps: Cut five 4½in (11.5cm) squares

Backing fabric: Cut five 7in (17.8cm) circles using the template

Fusible woven interlining: Cut five 8½in (21.6cm) squares

Fusible foam interlining: Cut five 4½in (11.5cm) squares

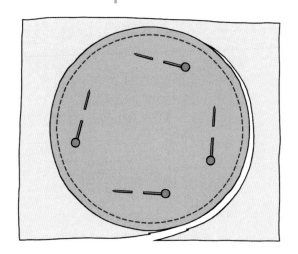

1 Place a backing fabric circle onto a woven interlining square, with the right side of the fabric facing the non-adhesive side of the interlining. Pin in place. Sew around the outer edge of the circle. Cut away the excess interlining around the circle, being careful not to cut into the stitching.

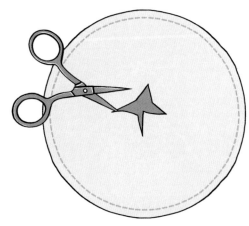

2 Use small sharp scissors to make two small cuts in the center of the interlining to make a cross. Be sure that only the interlining is cut and not the background fabric.

3 Carefully turn the whole circle to the right side through the cuts in the center. Take care not to rip the cuts. Work around the edge of the circle to push out the seams. Use a Hera marker or knitting needle to carefully center the seam along the edge of the fabric.

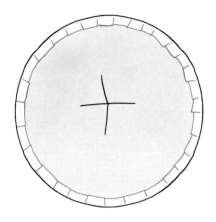

4 Press around the whole circle, ensuring that the woven interlining isn't visible around the seams on the fabric side. The interlining is translucent, so you will be able to see the seam allowance on the inside of the piece, as in this illustration. As you press the circle, the cut center of the interlining will be pressed closed. Repeat steps 1–4 to create all five background circles and set them aside.

5 Position a print cotton square wrong side down onto the fusible side of a foam interlining square and cover with a pressing cloth. Press using a press-and-lift motion, rather than sweeping movements, to keep the fabric wrinkle-free. Repeat to fuse all five print-cotton fabric squares onto the foam interlining squares.

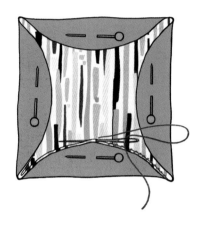

6 Place a background circle with the interlining uppermost. Position a fused foam square on the center of the circle, with the print cotton uppermost. Fold each side of the background fabric onto the square. Check that all the folded sections are even and pin in place. With a needle and thread, sew each folded section in place using ladder stitch (see page 124) along the inside of the fold to keep the stitches discreet. Alternatively, you can use a sewing machine to sew each section into place. Repeat to sew all five squares.

7 Arrange the squares with one in the center (this will become the base of the tub) and the remaining squares around each of its sides.

TIPS

When working with fusible foam, be sure to place the fabric onto the fusible side. It can be hard to tell which side of the foam has the adhesive, so run the tip of a pin across both sides—the one that feels rougher is the side with the adhesive.

This design is great for showcasing pretty print fabrics, you can even fussy cut (see page 17) a particular motif or element for the center of each square. If you have used a directional print, as I have done, be sure to check each square will be the right way up on the finished box before you join the seams.

8 Using a needle and thread, join the panels where they meet using small ladder stitches. Alternatively, you can sew these seams with a sewing machine using zigzag stitch. Fold up the sides and join them in the same way to make the tub.

Finishing

Trim any excess threads and press the tub lightly to neaten. You can fill the inside of the tub with batting (wadding) while you press it to help keep the squares neat.

hexi-accent needlebook

A needlebook is a lovely addition to your sewing supplies, and making your own allows you to use your favorite fabrics and colors from your stash. The hexagons in this project are created using English Paper Piecing, so this mini make is a great way to try out this technique.

FABRIC AND MATERIALS

Cotton fabric scraps in a selection of prints

Linen fabric scraps

White felt scrap

Cotton main fabric, 6¼ x 8½in (16 x 21.6cm)

Cotton lining fabric, 6¼ x 8½in (16 x 21.6cm)

Medium-loft fusible batting (wadding), Vlieseline H640, 6 x 8½in (15 x 21.6cm)

Ribbons or trims (for the inside of the needlebook)

Two pieces of ribbon, each 10in (25cm), for the ties

Coordinating thread

Piece of paper

TOOLS AND EQUIPMENT

Basic quilting kit (see page 6)

Glue stick

TEMPLATES (SEE PAGE 125)

Hexi-accent paper hexagon

Hexi-accent fussy cutting (optional, see tip)

FINISHED MEASUREMENTS

Closed: 6¾in (17cm) tall x 4in (10cm) wide

Open: 6¾in (17cm) tall x 8in (20cm) wide

CUTTING INSTRUCTIONS

Paper: Cut four hexagons using the paper hexagon template

1 Place one of the paper hexagons onto the wrong side of a fabric scrap. Using a rotary cutter and ruler, cut around the template, leaving a ¼in (0.5cm) fabric border around each side of the paper hexagon. Fold each side of the fabric over the paper, finger-pressing until all sides have been folded neatly. Using a dab of glue or long hand-basting (tacking) stitches to secure. Repeat for the remaining hexagon pieces so you have four in total.

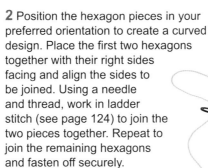

2 Position the hexagon pieces in your preferred orientation to create a curved design. Place the first two hexagons together with their right sides facing and align the sides to be joined. Using a needle and thread, work in ladder stitch (see page 124) to join the two pieces together. Repeat to join the remaining hexagons and fasten off securely.

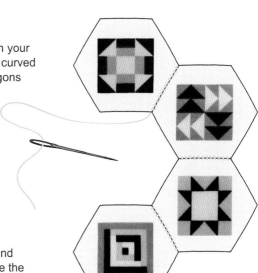

3 Remove the backing papers and press the hexagons neatly. Place the hexagons into position on the right side of the main fabric, on what will be the front of the needlebook. When you're happy with the placement, pin the hexagons in place.

4 With a needle and thread, carefully stitch around the outer edges of the hexagons to secure them in place on the main fabric. Work with small ladder stitches for a discreet finish.

5 Place the main fabric with its wrong side facing up. Position the fusible batting on top with its adhesive side facing the fabric. The batting will be slightly smaller than the fabric so ensure that the border around each side is even. Use an iron to fuse neatly into place and allow to cool.

TIPS

The fabrics for these hexagons have been "fussy cut," meaning a section of the print is deliberately cut in a way to showcase it. You can either use a clear template to cut the hexagons, or you can use the fussy cutting template which is ¼in (0.5cm) larger on each side than the desired hexagon. Carefully cut away the inner hexagon of the fussy cutting template. Position the opening on the fabric so you can see the section you

wish to cut, then draw around the outer edge of the fussy cutting template. Remove the template and cut the piece from the fabric.

English Paper Piecing involves folding fabrics around paper templates. Once the fabrics are sewn into place, the papers are removed. The template needs to be secured temporarily to the fabric while you work the project—you can either glue it in place or you can tack it in place with a needle and thread.

If you wish to reuse the paper templates, use a hole punch to make a small hole in the center of each template. This makes it easier to release them from the project without damage, for future use.

6 Place the lining fabric with its right side facing up. Trim two pieces of linen with pinking shears and layer them in size order, adding in any ribbon accents if desired (I added a small piece of ribbon with a scissors motif). Pin into place on the left-hand side of the lining fabric. Machine-sew in place along the top edge of the linen and ribbon piece. Use a length of Bondaweb to secure a length of ribbon across the length of the lining to conceal the stitching. Trim the felt scrap using pinking shears and fold it to create two layers so that one edge is slightly longer. Pin in your desired position on the right-hand side of the lining. Machine-sew the folded felt panel in place.

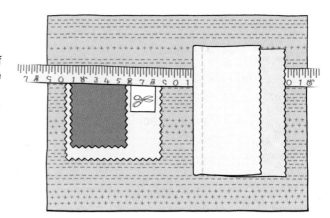

7 Place the main fabric with its right side facing up. Place the end of a ribbon tie in the center of one of the short sides. Sew in place, within the ¼in (0.5cm) seam allowance. Repeat with the second ribbon tie on the other short side.

8 Pin the ribbon ties away from the edge of the fabric. Place the lining and main fabrics together with their right sides facing, and pin or clip in place.

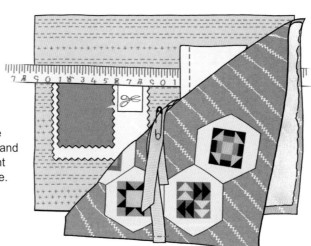

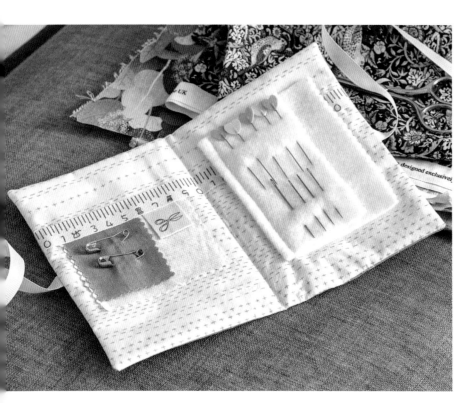

9 Sew the lining and main fabric pieces together around the edge, using the edge of the batting as a guide. Leave a 2½in (6.5cm) gap in the seam. Carefully clip the excess seam allowance fabric at the corners (see page 119).

10 Turn the piece to the right side through the gap in the seam. Push out the corners fully, using a knitting needle or similar as needed. Press the seam allowance along the gap inwards and hand-sew the gap closed with a needle and thread using ladder stitch.

Finishing
Trim any excess threads and press lightly to neaten.

notebook pen holder

Keeping a pen handy is a must for stationery addicts, and this handy pouch for your writing tools will help to take your journaling to the next level. With its elastic strap you can secure this to your notebook so it is always right where you need it!

FABRIC AND MATERIALS

Cotton fabric scraps in a selection of prints

Cotton main fabric, 3½ x 8in (9 x 20cm)

Cotton backing fabric, 3½ x 8in (9 x 20cm)

Batting (wadding), 3½ x 8in (9 x 20cm)

Fusible woven interlining, Vlieseline G700, 7 x 10in (18 x 25.5cm)

Coordinating thread

Elastic, 11in (28cm) long and ¾in (2cm) wide

TOOLS AND EQUIPMENT

Basic quilting kit (see page 6)

Spray adhesive (optional)

FINISHED MEASUREMENTS

3in (7.5cm) wide x 7½in (19cm) long

TIP

This notebook pen holder can be customized to accommodate your preferred writing accessories. Increase the width of the panels to make a wider pouch to stow more stationery supplies.

CUTTING INSTRUCTIONS

Print cotton fabric scraps: Cut two 3½ x 10in (9 x 25.4cm) pieces, for Pockets A and B

Fusible woven interlining: Cut two 3½ x 10in (9 x 25.4cm) pieces

1 Place the batting onto the wrong side of the main fabric. You can spray baste it in place if desired (see tip on page 55).

2 With a ruler and a Hera or crease marker, mark out some quilting lines evenly across the surface of the fabric. Working with a contrast thread and a stitch length of ⅛in (3mm), sew the quilting lines across the fabric and batting.

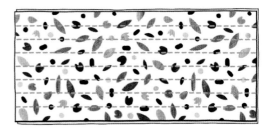

3 Fuse a piece of interlining onto the wrong side of the pocket A fabric (which will be the large pocket) and allow to cool. Fold the pocket piece in half with the wrong sides together, aligning the short ends. Press and set aside.

4 Fuse the interlining onto the wrong side of the pocket B fabric (which will be the small pocket) and allow to cool.

5 Fold the pocket B piece in half with the right sides facing and align the short ends. Mark a point 2in (5cm) from the raw short end. Using a ruler and erasable marker, mark a diagonal line across the piece from this point. Sew along the marked line. Using a rotary cutter and ruler, trim away the excess fabric, leaving ¼in (0.5cm) seam allowance from the stitches.

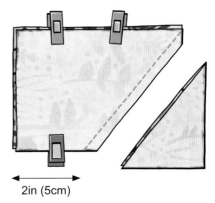

2in (5cm)

6 Turn the pocket B piece to the right side and press. Topstitch (see page 119) along the diagonal folded section, ⅛in (3mm) from the fold.

7 Place the quilted piece with the right side facing up. Position Pocket A (the larger pocket) onto the lower part and place Pocket B (the smaller pocket) on top. Align all the raw edges along the sides and base. Pin or clip in place.

TIP
Sewing the elastic in place inside the seam allowance will hold it in place while you construct the holder, and means you won't need to navigate sewing around lots of pins!

8 Place the length of elastic onto the right side of the holder. Place each end of the elastic in the center of each short side of the holder, aligning the raw edges and making sure the elastic isn't twisted. Pin in place. Sew each end of the elastic in place within the ¼in (0.5cm) seam allowance.

9 Tuck the elastic away from the edge, either into the pocket or in the center of the main section with a safety pin. Place the backing fabric on top of the holder with the right sides facing and pin or clip into place.

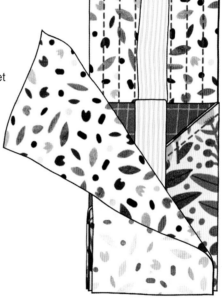

10 Sew around all four sides of the holder, leaving a 2in (5cm) gap in the top of one long side (away from the pockets). Carefully clip away the excess seam allowance at the corners (see page 119).

11 Turn the pen holder to the right side through the gap in the seam. Push out the corners neatly and roll all the seams so they are on the very edge of the holder and not visible on each side. Press the seam allowance at the gap inwards and hand-sew the gap closed with a needle and thread using ladder stitch (see page 124).

Finishing
Trim any excess threads and press lightly to neaten.

baby bib

This bib is both cute and frugal, working with offcuts of pretty print cottons. The fabrics are placed onto the batting and sewn into place to create the patchwork design. Whether you're making this for your own little one or to give as a gift, this is a great project to personalize.

FABRIC AND MATERIALS

Cotton fabric scraps in a selection of prints

Cotton backing fabric, 15in (38cm) square

Batting (wadding), 15in (38cm) square

Coordinating thread

TOOLS AND EQUIPMENT

Basic quilting kit (see page 6)

Heat- or water-erasable marker

Pinking shears

KAM snap and tool (or use your preferred fastenings)

TEMPLATE (SEE PAGE 125)

Baby bib (Sizes: Newborn, 3–6 months, and 6 months plus)

FINISHED MEASUREMENTS

Newborn: 10in (25cm) long x 8¾in (22cm) wide. Neck opening: 3¼in (8.5cm) wide

3–6 months: 12¼in (31cm) long x 10¾in (27.5cm) wide. Neck opening: 4⅜in (11cm) wide

6 months plus: 13¾in (35cm) long x 12¾in (32cm) wide. Neck opening: 5⅛in (13cm) wide

CUTTING INSTRUCTIONS

Print cotton fabric scraps: Cut a selection of strips, each long enough to cover the width of your chosen template with at least ⅜in (1cm) extra on either side, and 2–2¾in (5–7cm) wide

1 Place the template onto the batting and draw around it to create a guide for the patchwork. Place the first strip onto the lower portion of the marked bib outline with the right side uppermost. Ensure that the fabric covers the width of the marked bib.

2 Place the second strip of fabric onto the first piece with the right sides facing—this will form the lowest strip on the bib. Ensure that the long raw edges of the fabrics are aligned and that the second strip covers the width of the bib. Pin in place. Sew the two pieces together to the batting along the lower edge. Press the fabrics open.

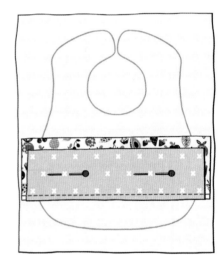

TIPS

This project can be easily customized or personalized with hand embroidery. Simply sew the recipient's name or a message onto one of the cotton strips with backstitch (see page 124) and colorful embroidery threads, before joining the strip into place.

This bib features a cotton backing but this could be substituted for a soft cotton toweling or jersey if preferred.

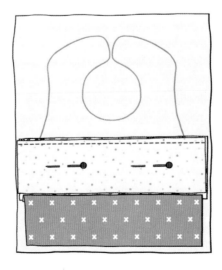

3 Position the next strip of fabric onto the first strip with the right sides facing. Ensure the fabrics cover the width of the marked bib outline and the long raw edges are aligned. Pin in place. Sew to join the two pinned pieces together to the batting. Press the fabrics open.

4 Repeat to cover the remaining sections of the bib. Where the upper portion of the bib forms the neck opening, you can work with two small pieces (as shown here) or one long strip. Join the pieces with two short seams if you're using two pieces of fabric (as here) or one long seam if using a long strip. Press the fabrics open.

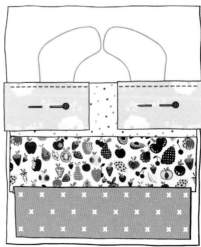

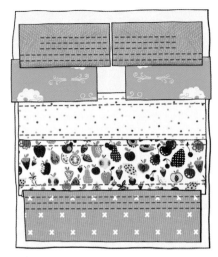

5 Repeat to add the remaining strips to cover the final section of the bib. Press the fabrics open. Sew quilting lines as desired to the surface of the bib. Here simple straight-line quilting has been worked to echo the joins in the pieces.

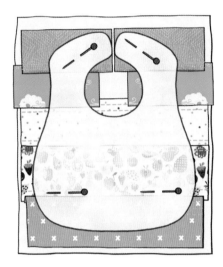

6 Reposition the bib template over the patchwork panel and pin in place. With sharp scissors, carefully cut around the template. Remove the pinned template.

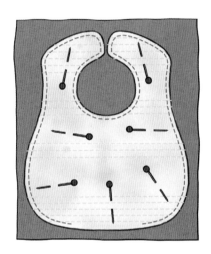

7 Place the quilted patchwork panel onto the backing fabric with their right sides facing and pin in place. Sew around the edge of the patchwork panel to join the front and backing fabric together. Leave a 2–3in (5–7.5cm) gap in the seam along the lower edge.

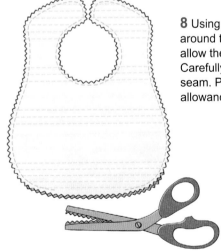

8 Using a pair of pinking shears, trim the seam allowance around the bib. This will not only reduce the bulk, but also allow the curved seams to sit more neatly on the finished piece. Carefully turn the bib to the right side through the gap in the seam. Push out all the seams and corners. Press the seam allowance along the gap inwards, and press the bib fully.

9 Hand-sew the gap closed using ladder stitch (see page 124). Place one part of the KAM snap or fastening onto one side of the neckline and follow the manufacturer's instructions to secure. Repeat to add the second part of the snap onto the other side of the bib to correspond with the first part.

Finishing
Trim any excess threads and press lightly to neaten.

pincushion

Pincushions are a sewing room staple and also make great gifts for like-minded creative friends. This pincushion features a Courthouse Steps block in the center and also has a small tab for you to store fabric clips.

FABRIC AND MATERIALS

Cotton fabric scraps in a selection of prints—light and dark shades

Cotton fabric scraps in a selection of solid colors—light and dark shades

Geometric fabric, 1 x 5in (2.5 x 12.7cm)

Cotton backing fabric, 5½in (14cm) square

Fusible woven interlining, Vlieseline G700, 1 x 5in (2.5 x 12.7cm)

Medium-loft fusible batting (wadding), Vlieseline H640, 5½in (14cm) square

Coordinating thread

Small amount of filling (see tip)

TOOLS AND EQUIPMENT

Basic quilting kit (see page 6)

FINISHED MEASUREMENTS

5in (13cm) square

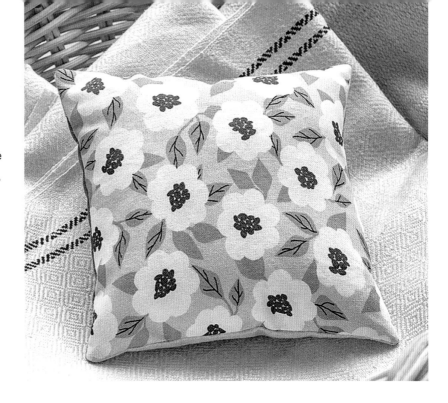

CUTTING INSTRUCTIONS

Print cotton fabric scraps:

Cut one 2in (5cm) square, for the center

Cut two 1 x 3in (2.5 x 7.5cm) pieces in dark fabrics, for round 1

Cut two 1 x 3½in (2.5 x 9cm) pieces in light fabrics, for round 1

Cut two 1 x 4in (2.5 x 10cm) pieces in dark fabrics, for round 2

Cut two 1 x 4½in (2.5 x 11.5cm) pieces in light fabrics, for round 2

Cut two 1¼ x 5in (3.2 x 12.7cm) pieces in dark fabrics, for round 3

Cut two 1¼ x 5½in (3.2 x 14cm) pieces in light fabrics, for round 3

TIPS

The Courthouse Steps is a traditional block and, similar to the Log Cabin Block, it is worked around a central square. For a Courthouse Steps block, the strips are added in pairs to opposite sides in turn, whereas in the Log Cabin they are worked around the block in a clockwise or counterclockwise manner.

You can fill your pincushion with fiberfill (stuffing) or fabric scraps and threads. You can also cut a kitchen scourer into small pieces and mix these with the fiberfill. Pushing pins and needles into this coarse material helps to keep them sharp.

1 Place the center square with its right side uppermost. Position the first round-1 shorter piece on the top edge with the right sides facing. Pin or clip and then sew in place.

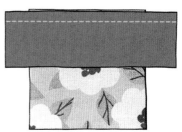

2 Press the fabric open and use a rotary cutter and ruler and mat to trim the excess fabric.

3 Repeat steps 1 and 2 to join the second round-1 shorter piece to the lower edge of the center square.

4 Rotate the piece so the two strips are on the right- and left-hand side edges. Place the first longer round-1 piece on the top edge with the right sides facing. Pin or clip and then sew in place. Press open and trim away the excess fabric. Repeat to sew the second longer round-1 piece to the bottom edge.

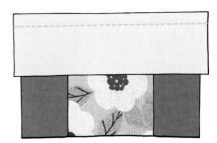

5 Continue in this manner, adding the round-2 shorter pieces and then the round-2 longer pieces to each side in turn, to create two r ounds of the Courthouse Steps block motif.

6 Use an iron to fuse a piece of interlining to the wrong side of the geometric strip—this will become the tab for holding the quilting clips. Allow to cool. Fold the strip in half with the wrong sides together. Align the long sides and press.

7 Place the geometric piece onto one side of the block, then place the first shorter round-3 on top, aligning the raw edges. Pin or clip and then sew in place. Press open. Sew the second shorter round-3 strip to the opposite side and press open.

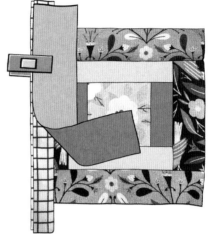

8 Add the final two longer round-3 pieces in the same manner and press the whole block neatly.

9 Position a piece of fusible batting onto the wrong side of the Courthouse Steps block, ensuring that the border around the edge is even. Using an iron, fuse in place and set aside to cool.

10 Place the bonded Courthouse Steps block onto the backing fabric with the right sides together and the raw edges aligned, and pin or clip in place.

11 Sew around each side, using the edge of the fusible batting as a guide. Leave a small gap of 2in (5cm) in the seam along one edge for turning through. Clip away the excess seam allowance on the corners (see page 119).

12 Turn the piece to the right side through the gap in the seam and carefully push out the corners. Press the seam allowance along the gap inward. Fill the pincushion with your choice of filling until firm.

13 Using a needle and thread, hand-sew the gap in the seam allowance closed with ladder stitch (see page 124).

Finishing
Trim any excess threads and press lightly to neaten.

notebook cover

Personalize your diary or journal with this pretty cover that includes a ribbon page marker to help keep your place. The cover slides onto the cover of the notebook, so you can replace the book and reuse the cover as many times as you like.

FABRIC AND MATERIALS

Cotton fabrics in a selection of prints

Low-volume cotton main fabric

Cotton lining fabric, 9¼ x 13in (23.5 x 33cm)

Medium-loft fusible batting (wadding), Vlieseline H640, 9¼ x 13in (23.5 x 33cm)

Coordinating thread

Ribbon, 11in (28cm) long

TOOLS AND EQUIPMENT

Basic quilting kit (see page 6)

Knitting needle (optional)

FINISHED MEASUREMENTS

Fits a Half Letter (A5) book

Closed: 8¾in (22cm) tall x 6¼in (16cm) wide

Open: 8¾in (22cm) tall x 12½in (32cm) wide

CUTTING INSTRUCTIONS

Print cotton fabric scraps: Cut five 2½ x 8in (6.5 x 20cm) strips

Low-volume cotton main fabric: Cut ten 2½ x 8in (6.5 x 20cm) strips

TIPS

This cover fits a standard Half Letter (A5) notebook, but you can upsize it to fit a larger book. Measure the book open to accommodate the spine, add 6in (15cm) to the width for the folded sections, and add ¼in (0.5cm) to each of the four sides for the seam allowances.

While this cover can be made with scrap strips of fabrics, you can also make it with the pre-cut pieces from a Jelly Roll (see page 5), too!

1 Place the five print strips in your preferred order. Place a low-volume strip on one of the print strips with the right sides facing, aligning a short end. Pin or clip in place, then sew along the short end. Press the seam allowance toward the darker fabric. Repeat to sew another low-volume strip to the other short end of the print fabric.

2 Repeat step 1 to make four more strips, so you have five in total. Arrange the strips in your desired manner—I staggered the print sections. Place the open book on the panel, aligning one short end. There should be around 7in (18cm) excess on the the other short end to ensure the panel will cover the book.

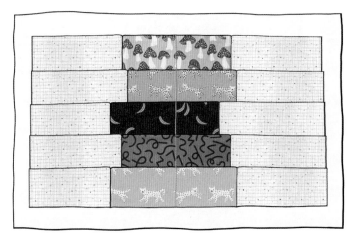

3 Join the strips by placing two together with their right sides facing and aligning the long raw edges. Pin or clip and then sew in place. Continue until all five strips are joined. Using a rotary cutter, ruler and mat, square off the panel neatly. Place the panel with its right side uppermost onto the fusible batting. Bond the panel in place with an iron and allow to cool. Mark the center line of the panel with an erasable marker.

4 Trim the completed panel to square off the sides and cut away the batting border using a rotary cutter and ruler.

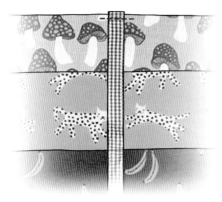

5 Pin the ribbon in place at the top of the panel on the center line. Sew in place, inside the ¼in (0.5cm) seam allowance.

6 Place the patchwork piece and the lining fabric together with their right sides facing, and pin or clip in place. Ensure that the ribbon is pinned away from the edges.

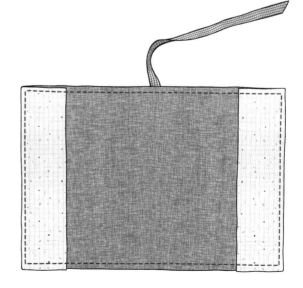

7 Sew around all four sides of the cover, leaving a 2in (5cm) gap in one side. Clip the bulk from the seam allowance at the corners (see page 119).

8 Carefully turn the cover to the right side through the gap in the seam. Use a knitting needle or poking tool to push out the corners neatly. Hand-sew the gap in the seam closed using ladder stitch (see page 124).

9 Press the cover fully. With the lining side uppermost, fold each short side toward the lining by 3in (7.5cm) and pin or clip in place. Sew around all four sides of the cover. This will secure the pockets at each end.

Finishing
Trim any excess threads and press lightly to neaten.

crayon roll

Pocket-sized and pretty, this mini holder is ideal for stowing a few crayons and paper. Whether you use it for entertaining little ones or keeping your to-do list to hand, this a quick and easy make that is practical, too.

FABRIC AND MATERIALS

Cotton fabrics in three prints
(I used a rainbow fabric and two
low-volume fabrics)

Low-loft fusible batting (wadding),
Vlieseline H630, 6 x 11¾in (15 x 29.8cm)

Coordinating thread

TOOLS AND EQUIPMENT

Basic quilting kit (see page 6)

Hera or crease marker

Hand-sewing needle

FINISHED MEASUREMENTS

Open: 4½in (11.5cm) tall x 8in
(20cm) wide

Closed: 4½in (11.5cm) tall x 4in
(10cm) wide

CUTTING INSTRUCTIONS

Fabric A (rainbow print): Cut one
4¾ x 12in (12 x 30cm) piece

Fabric B (low-volume): Cut one
1¾ x 12in (4.5 x 30cm) piece

Fabric C (low-volume, for the
lining): Cut one 6¼ x 12in
(16 x 30cm) piece

TIPS

When sewing sections where the fabric and batting are doubled, you may prefer to change to a walking foot on your sewing machine. This will help the thicker layers of fabric feed through your machine smoothly and help keep the stitches even.

This holder can be scaled up to accommodate more pencils and larger paper—simply create the quilted rectangle to your preferred size before folding and stitching.

1 Place the Fabric A and Fabric B strips together with the right sides facing, and align the raw top edges. Pin or clip in place.

2 Sew the fabrics together along the top edge.

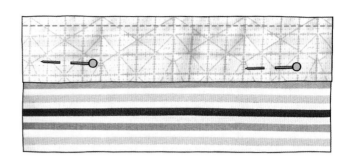

3 Press the seam toward the darker of the two fabrics. Place the fusible batting top, with its fusible side facing the wrong side of the fabric. The batting is slightly smaller, so there should be a ¼in (0.5cm) border around each side. Cover with a pressing cloth and fuse neatly into place. Leave to cool fully.

4 Place the Fabric C lining piece and the outer piece together with the right sides facing and the edges neatly aligned. Pin or clip into place.

5 Sew the lining and the outer fabrics together, using the edge of the fusible batting as a guide. Leave a 2–3in (5–7.5cm) gap in one long side. Use small sharp scissors to trim the corners, being careful not to snip into the stitches (see page 119).

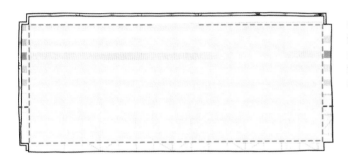

6 Turn the piece to the right side through the gap in the seam. Press the seam allowance along the gap. With a needle and thread, close the gap using ladder stitch (see page 124).

7 With the lining side uppermost, find the center of each long side and join them with a Hera or crease marker. Fold over the short left-hand side to make a 2in (5cm) wide pocket and pin or clip in place. Using a water or heat-erasable marker and ruler, mark out two lines for stitching spaced 2in (5cm) apart. Sew these using a straight machine stitch working carefully over the folded section.

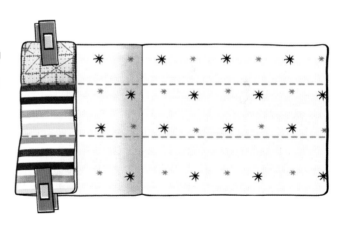

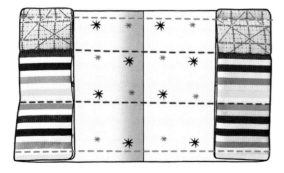

8 Fold over the right-hand short side to make a second 2in (5cm) wide pocket and pin or clip in place. Sew along the top and bottom edges to secure the two pockets.

Finishing
Trim any excess threads and press lightly to neaten.

dino taggie lovey

This dinosaur motif comforter has a ribbon edge, making it a tactile treat for babies and small children. Finished with dimple cuddle fleece backing fabric, this mini blanket is super soft and snuggly.

FABRIC AND MATERIALS

Cotton fabric scraps in a selection of prints—two pink and three green (five prints in total)

Print-cotton fabric for dino

Dimple cuddle fleece, 13in (33cm) square, for the backing

Ricrac, pink

Ribbon lengths

Medium-loft fusible batting (wadding), Vlieseline H640, 20 x 13in (51 x 33cm)

Fusible adhesive, Vlieseline Bondaweb

Coordinating thread

TOOLS AND EQUIPMENT

Basic quilting kit (see page 6)

Fabric glue

Hand-sewing needle

Embroidery thread or fabric marker for face details

TEMPLATE (SEE PAGE 125)

Dino appliqué template

FINISHED MEASUREMENTS

12in (30cm) square, excluding the ribbon tabs

NOTES

• Always monitor babes and small children with blankets, quilts, and comforters.

• Ensure that the face, if sewn on, is fully secure to avoid any hazards to children.

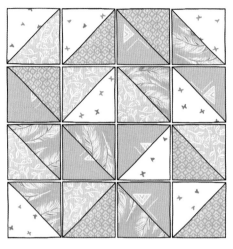

1 Place two of the print squares together with the right sides facing and follow steps 1–3 on page 122 to make two Half Square Triangles (HST). Press the seam allowance over to the darker fabric. Using a rotary cutter, ruler, and mat, trim the excess seam allowance and square to 3½in (9cm). Repeat to create 16 HST in total. These can be chain-pieced (see page 123), by working the first line of stitching on each square, then snipping the chain of thread and working the second line on each of the squares. Arrange the squares into four rows of four squares. Move the squares around until you are happy with the placement.

2 Working with two squares at a time and placing them right sides together, follow steps 2–4 on page 121 to join the squares to make four rows and press the seams in alternate directions. Follow step 5 on page 121 to join the rows together, neatly nesting (see page 120) the seam allowances. Press the whole quilt top to neaten.

CUTTING INSTRUCTIONS

Print cotton fabric scraps: Cut sixteen 3⅞in (3.8cm) squares

Medium-loft fusible batting: Cut one 13in (33cm) square and one 7in (17.8cm) square

TIP

This quilt top is made with Half Square Triangles (HST). There are a number of ways to make half-square triangles. Here they are made by cutting squares larger than required for the finished square, placing them right sides together and stitching either side of the central diagonal line. Once cut down the diagonal line, this yields two Half Square Triangles at once.

3 Place the large fusible batting square with the adhesive side uppermost. Place the quilt top on top with its right side uppermost. Cover with a pressing cloth and fuse the batting to the wrong side of the quilt top. Take the quilt to the sewing machine and quilt as desired. Here, straight-line quilting has been worked following the seams to create a grid design.

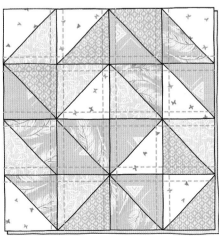

4 Place the Dino template onto the small piece of fusible batting and carefully cut it out. Place the fusible batting onto the wrong side of the print-cotton dino fabric, with the adhesive side facing the wrong side of the fabric. Cover with a pressing cloth and fuse in place. Trim the excess fabric to leave a ½in (1.3cm) border around the fusible batting. Clip the seam allowance around the curves (see page 119).

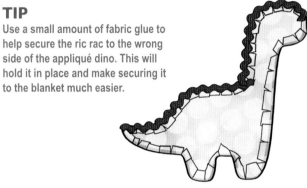

TIP

Use a small amount of fabric glue to help secure the ric rac to the wrong side of the appliqué dino. This will hold it in place and make securing it to the blanket much easier.

5 Fold the seam allowance over to the wrong side of the batting and press into place using a small amount of fabric glue to secure. Position a length of ric rac along the top of the dinosaur, so the top edge of the ric rac will be visible on the right side of the dinosaur. Use fabric glue to secure the ric rac into position. Using the template, cut out a dino motif from the Bondaweb. Fuse the Bondaweb to the wrong side of the dinosaur motif. Once cooled, remove the backing paper.

6 Position the dino appliqué motif onto the quilt top as desired. Using a pressing cloth and iron, fuse it into place on the quilt top. With a hand-sewing needle and coordinating cotton, work around the outer edge of the dino motif to secure it to the quilt using ladder stitch (see page 124).

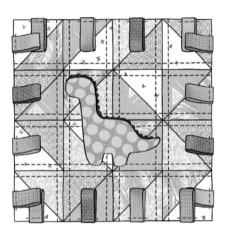

7 Cut the ribbons into 4in (10cm) pieces and fold each one in half. Position them around the outer edge of the quilt and pin or clip into place. Secure the ribbon tags to the quilt top by sewing them in position using a ⅛in (3mm) seam allowance.

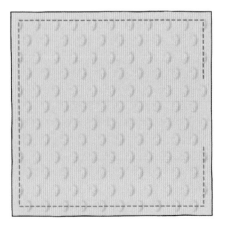

8 Place the piece of dimple cuddle fleece backing onto the quilt top with the right sides facing and the raw edges aligned. Pin or clip in place. Sew around all four sides, leaving a 2–3in (5–7.5cm) gap in the seam for turning through. Clip into the seam allowance at the corners to reduce the bulk (see page 119).

9 Turn the blanket through to the right side. Tuck the seam allowance along the gap to the inside and press the blanket fully. Topstitch (see page 119) around the outer edge of the blanket, increasing the stitch length to 3 and taking a ¼in (0.5cm) seam allowance.

10 Using a fabric marker or embroidery thread, add the facial features to the dino motif.

Finishing

Trim any excess threads and press lightly to neaten.

rainbow banner

This appliqué banner is great for using up leftover pieces of your favorite print fabrics. You can also personalize the design by embroidering a name or motto around the rainbow. The metal eyelet rings give the banner a modern look and allow it to be hung neatly on hooks or nails. You could also thread a piece of cord through the rings to hang up the banner.

FABRIC AND MATERIALS

Cotton fabric scraps in a selection of prints in three colors

Cotton main fabric, 9 x 13in (23 x 33cm)

Cotton backing fabric, 9 x 13in (23 x 33cm)

Medium-loft fusible batting (wadding), Vlieseline H640, 9 x 13in (23 x 33cm)

Fusible adhesive, Vlieseline Bondaweb

Perle cotton thread

Coordinating thread

TOOLS AND EQUIPMENT

Basic quilting kit (see page 6)

½in (15cm) metal eyelets, punch tool, and hammer (see tip on page 47)

Hand-sewing needle

TEMPLATES (SEE PAGE 127)

Rainbow banner appliqué motif

Rainbow banner pennant

FINISHED MEASUREMENTS

10½in (26.6cm) tall (to point) x 7in (17.8cm) wide

CUTTING INSTRUCTIONS

Main fabric and backing fabric: Cut the pennant shape from each fabric using the template. If you are using the same fabric for the front and back, fold the fabric and cut two pieces at once.

Medium-loft fusible batting: Cut the pennant shape using the template

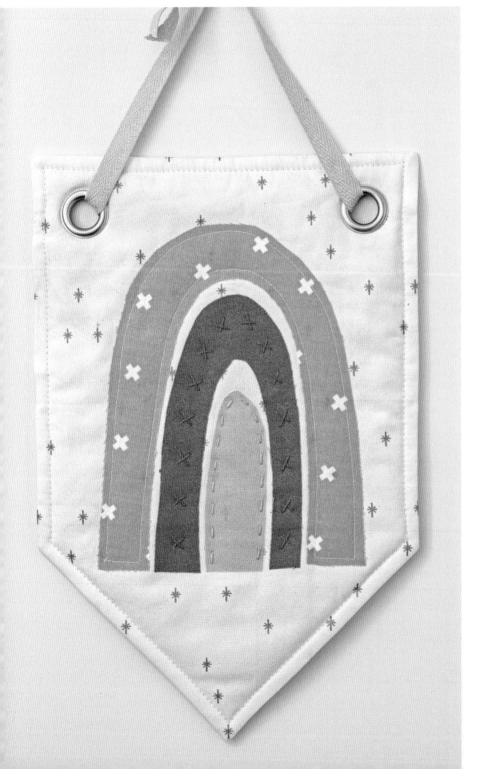

1 Fuse a selection of fabric scraps onto a piece of Bondaweb. Allow to cool and leave the paper backing in place. Draw around each of the rainbow appliqué motif templates onto the paper-backing side of the fabrics, then cut them out.

2 Using a rotary cutter, ruler, and cutting mat, trim the fusible batting pennant piece by ¼in (0.5cm) on each side.

TIP

You can increase the size or length of the banner by adapting the template. Use a photocopier to enlarge the whole template, or make the template longer and keep the width the same.

3 Place the main fabric pennant piece with its wrong side uppermost. With the fusible side down, place the batting on the wrong side of the main fabric piece. The batting will be ¼in (0.5cm) smaller than the fabric, so ensure that the border is even on each side. Cover the project with a pressing cloth and bond in place with an iron.

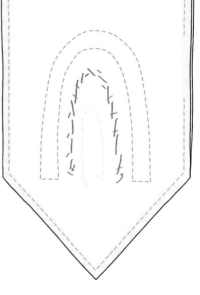

4 Once the batting has cooled, place the rainbow design in your desired position on the right side of the front pennant piece. Remove the backing paper from the Bondaweb. Fuse the rainbow design in place using the iron.

5 Thread a needle with perle cotton and work a selection of long running stitches and cross stitches (see page 124) over the inner two pieces of the rainbow design. Use a sewing machine and a stitch length of ⅛in (3mm) to sew around the edge of the outer rainbow piece.

6 With the right sides facing, place the front and back banner panels together. Align the raw edges and pin or clip in place.

7 Sew the pieces together, using the batting as a guide. Leave a 3in (7.5cm) gap in one side.

8 Clip the excess seam allowance fabric at the corners and the point (see page 119), ensuring that you don't cut the stitches. Turn the work through to the right side through the gap in the seam and press.

9 Topstitch (see page 119) around the outer edge, ¼in (0.5cm) from the edge and using a stitch size of 3. Mark the placement for the metal eyelets on either side of the banner, ½in (1.3cm) from the edges. Follow the manufacturer's instructions to secure the metal eyelets into place.

Finishing
Trim any excess threads and press lightly to neaten.

TIP
Metal eyelets rings require the use of a specialist tool and a hammer to secure them in place. The tool usually comes packaged with the hardware, but be sure to check. If you've not applied eyelets before, have a practice run on a scrap of fabric so you can master the technique before you add the eyelets to your finished piece.

chapter 2
bags & pouches

small folded wallet

This wallet is made as a single piece that is folded to make two pockets, so it's roomy enough for your cards and essentials. The patchwork panel is made with interlining using a fuse-and-fold technique, so it's great for even the smallest squares.

FABRIC AND MATERIALS

Cotton fabric scraps in a selection of prints—2 pink and three green, five prints in total

Lightweight fusible interlining, Vlieseline F220, 20 x 20in (50.8 x 50.8cm)

Cotton backing fabric, 8 x 14in (20 x 35.5cm)

Coordinating thread

1 KAM snap or snap fastening, ½in (1.3cm) in diameter

TOOLS AND EQUIPMENT

Basic quilting kit (see page 6)

TEMPLATE (SEE PAGE 125)

Small folded wallet

FINISHED MEASUREMENTS

3in x 5½in (7.5 x 14cm), when closed

CUTTING INSTRUCTIONS

Print cotton fabric scraps: Cut fourteen 2½in (6.5cm) squares

1 Place the interlining with the fusible side uppermost. Lay out the squares, right side up, onto the interlining to create two rows of six squares, and then add a top row with two squares placed centrally. Cover with a pressing cloth and use an iron to carefully fuse the squares onto the interlining. Be careful not to accidentally fuse any interlining onto the pressing cloth—you can trim away the excess interlining before you fuse the pieces if you prefer.

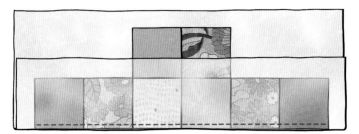

2 Once the interlining has cooled and the fabrics are fully bonded, fold the bottom row up onto the middle row with the right sides together. Pin or clip in place. Sew along the fold.

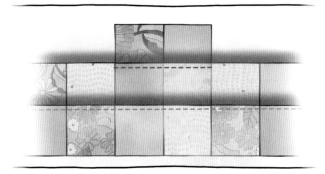

3 Open out the piece so the bottom row doesn't get in the way for this step. Repeat step 2 to fold the middle row up onto the top row with the right sides together. Sew along the fold. Open out the piece and place it right-side down.

TIPS

The fuse-and-fold technique is great for getting really neat seams when joining squares. You can work with squares of any size—as long as all the pieces are cut and placed precisely before fusing, the quilted panel will be neat and quick to make.

This wallet is secured with a KAM snap, but you can always add a ribbon loop and button if you prefer.

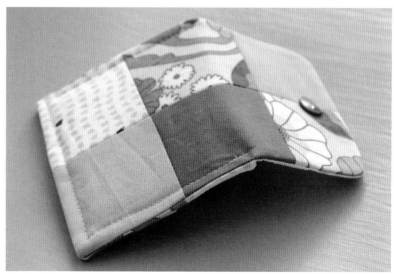

4 Using small sharp scissors, cut along the fold of the top section (see step 5 on page 80) and press the seam allowance open. Repeat to cut along the fold of the lower folded section and press the seam allowance open (see page 119).

5 Follow step 2 to fold and then sew along each of the vertical seams. Follow step 4 to cut along each of the vertical folds and press all the seams open.

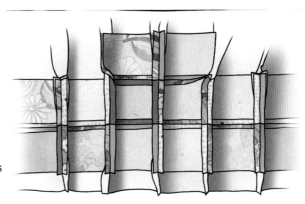

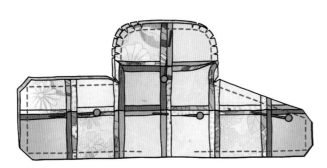

6 Place the backing fabric with the right side uppermost. Place the patchwork panel on top with the right side facing down. Place the Folded Wallet template on top of the fabrics and pin in place. Draw around the template onto the fabric. Sew directly on the drawn line, leaving a 2in (5cm) gap in the bottom edge for turning through. Trim around the wallet, leaving a ¼in (0.5cm) border around the stitching. Trim the corners and clip into the seam allowance around the curves to reduce bulk (see page 119).

7 Turn the wallet to the right side by pulling the fabric out through the gap in the stitching. Fold in the seam allowance along the gap and press the whole piece.

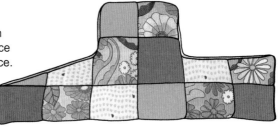

8 Turn the piece over so the lining side is uppermost. Fold the left-hand side section in to cover the central section. Then fold the right-hand side section in to cover the central section. Pin or clip in place. Increase the stitch length to 3. Sew down each side and along the lower edge. Secure a KAM snap or snap fastener to the flap of the wallet and repeat to add the corresponding part to the lower section of the wallet. Make sure that the two sides of the snap will match up before you secure them in place.

Finishing
Trim any excess threads and press lightly to neaten.

scrappy boxy pouch

There are always going to be some fabrics that you simply can't part with, even if they're the smallest scraps. So this stunning and practical zipper boxy pouch is a great opportunity to raid your precious scraps basket to create the patchwork panel.

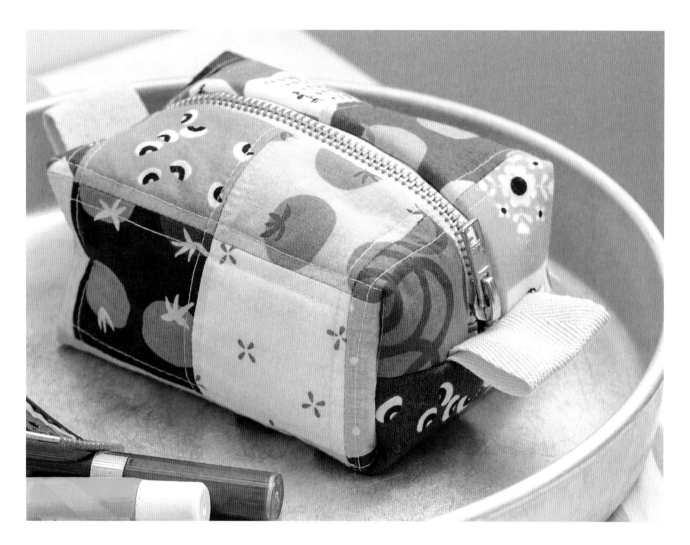

FABRIC AND MATERIALS

Cotton fabric scraps in a selection of prints

Cotton lining fabric, 12 x 15in (30 x 38cm)

Batting (wadding), 14 x 17in (35.5 x 43.2cm)

Lightweight fusible interlining, Vlieseline F220, 14 x 17in (35.5 x 43.2cm)

Coordinating thread

Zipper, 7in (18cm)

Two 4in (10cm) pieces of cotton webbing, 2in (5cm) wide

TOOLS AND EQUIPMENT

Basic quilting kit (see page 6)

Spray adhesive (optional)

FINISHED MEASUREMENTS

5in (13cm) long x 4in (10cm) deep x 2½in (6.5cm) tall

CUTTING INSTRUCTIONS

Print cotton fabric scraps: Cut twenty-two 2½in (6.5cm) squares

TIP

Seaming lots of small squares into pairs, rows, and finally a panel can be time consuming, especially when you are trying to match all the seams neatly. Using a piece of interlining to fuse the small squares into place before folding and stitching is a quick and precise way to get a neat and square panel.

1 Place the lightweight fusible interlining with its fusible side uppermost. Arrange the fabric squares into four rows of six squares on top. Place the squares neatly, using a ruler or mat to ensure they are in straight lines, and check they are not overlapping.

2 Use an iron to carefully fuse the fabrics into place. Set aside for about 30 minutes for the interlining to cool and the adhesive to fully bond.

3 Follow steps 3–5 on pages 79–80 of the Heart Talk Mini Quilt to sew all the seams of the four-square rows, then cut and press each seam allowance open.

4 Follow steps 6–7 on page 80 to sew the seams of the six-square rows, then cut and press each seam allowance open.

5 Lightly spray one side of the batting with adhesive. With right side uppermost, position the scrappy panel on top and press lightly to baste (tack) the layers together (see tip on page 55).

6 Quilt the panel either by hand or machine— here the panel is quilted using straight line stitching either side of the seams. Trim away the excess batting.

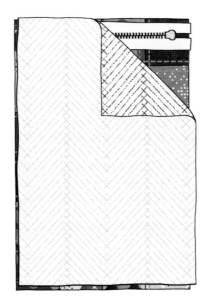

7 Place the scrappy panel with the right side uppermost. Position the zipper, right side down, on the panel, aligning the edge of tape with the raw edge of the fabric. The zipper teeth should be facing the fabric. Pin, clip, or glue-baste the zipper in place. Place the lining on top with the right sides facing and the raw edges aligned. With a zipper foot, secure the first side of the zipper in place, moving the zipper pull as needed to secure the whole length of the tape.

8 Press the scrappy panel and lining away from the zipper along the seam you've just sewn. Fold the scrappy panel with its right sides facing and align the second side of the zipper tape with the panel's raw edge. Then bring the lining over to cover the zipper tape. The quilted panel will be folded so its right sides are facing and the lining will be folded so its right sides are facing. Pin, clip, or glue-baste in place. With the zipper foot, sew along the raw edge to secure the second side of the zipper tape to the fabric and the lining.

9 You will now have a tube shape made from the lining and a tube shape made from the scrappy panel, with the zipper between the two sections. Roll the lining inside the scrappy panel section, position the seam along the center, and finger press in place. Fold each of the webbing pieces in half and pin one at the center of each end of the zipper. Sew the webbing tabs in place within the ¼in (0.5cm) seam allowance.

10 Turn the whole project through, so that the lining is outermost.

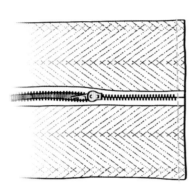

11 With the zipper partially open and positioned in the center, sew along each short end in turn.

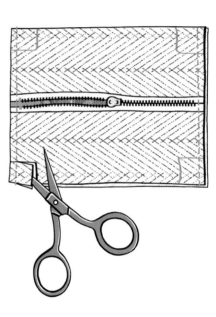

12 Use a ruler and pen or pencil to mark out a 1in (2.5cm) square at each of the corners. Carefully cut each corner away.

13 Open out one corner, align the cut edges, and pin or clip in place. Sew along the cut edges, clip away the excess, and zigzag stitch the seam allowance to neaten as desired. Repeat to make the remaining boxed corners.

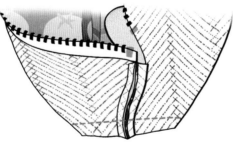

14 Turn the pouch through the open zipper and push out the corners neatly.

Finishing
Trim any excess threads and press lightly to neaten.

TIPS
Sewing in a zipper needn't be stressful. Remember to switch to a zipper foot to help you align the stitches carefully. Glue-basting the zipper in place can make sewing easier as you won't have to navigate pins or clips while you sew.

When spray basting, spray the adhesive onto the batting and press the fabrics on top—this will prevent any blobs of adhesive showing from through on the right side of the fabric.

drawstring bag

This versatile drawstring bag can be used for so many different purposes, from wrapping a special gift to organizing your holiday suitcase. Converting a simple patchwork panel into a pretty drawstring bag is a quick and easy project, plus it can be scaled up or down to any size you like!

FABRIC AND MATERIALS

Cotton fabric scraps in a selection of solid pink shades

Print cotton, for the lower panel

Print cotton, for the channels

Lining fabric

Coordinating thread

Perle cotton thread

Two pieces of cotton twill tape, each 26¾in (68cm)

Two cord stops

TOOLS AND EQUIPMENT

Basic quilting kit (see page 6)

Safety pin

FINISHED MEASUREMENTS

8½in (21.6cm) tall x 8in (20cm) wide

CUTTING INSTRUCTIONS

Cotton fabric scraps in solid colors: Cut 24 x 2½in (6.5cm) squares

Print cotton: Cut two 2½ x 8½in (6.5 x 21.6cm) pieces, for the lower panels

Print cotton: Cut two 2 x 8½in (5 x 21.6cm) pieces, for the channels

Lining fabric: Cut two 8½ x 9in (21.6 x 22.8cm) pieces

TIP

This panel is made by joining squares, first into pairs and then rows. The rows are then joined together to complete the panel. You can chain-piece (see page 123) these elements if you prefer, to make the project quicker.

1 Lay out the pink fabric squares into three rows of four squares and move them around until you're happy with the placement.

2 Sew the first two squares in the top row together (see page 121). Repeat to sew the second two squares in the top row together. Press the seams toward the left-hand side.

3 Place the two pairs right sides together and pin or clip in place. Sew together to make a row and press the seam toward the left-hand side. Repeat steps 2 and 3 to make two more rows in the same manner, alternating the direction the seam allowances are pressed on each row (see page 121).

4 Place the top and middle row together with the right sides facing and aligning the raw edges. The seams should nest neatly at the joins (see page 120). Pin or clip in place and sew together. Repeat to join the final row. Press the seam allowances downwards. Repeat steps 1–4 to make a second patchwork panel.

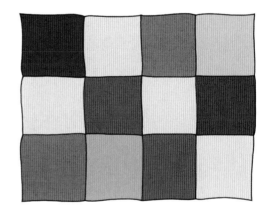

5 Place a lower panel on the lower edge of a patchwork panel with the right sides facing. Pin or clip in place and then sew along the lower edge. Press open and press the seam allowance downward. Repeat to add the second lower section to the second patchwork panel.

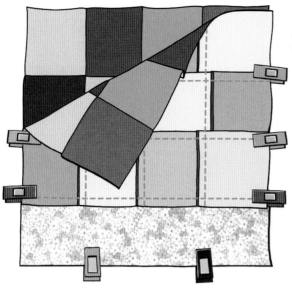

6 Place the two panels together with the right sides facing. Align the raw edges and the seams along each side. Pin or clip in place along the sides and the lower edge.

7 Sew along one long side, across the base, and along the second long side, leaving the top short side unstitched. Use small sharp scissors to carefully cut away the bulk at the corners (see page 119). Turn the bag to the right side.

8 Place the two lining pieces together with the right sides facing and the raw edges aligned. Pin or clip in place. Sew along one long side, across the base, and along the second long side, leaving a 2–3in (5–7.5cm) gap in the center of the seam at the base for turning through.

9 Take one of the channel fabric strips. Fold one of its short ends to the wrong side by ¼in (0.5cm) and press, then fold it to the wrong side again by ¼in (0.5cm) and press. Sew in place to secure the fold. Repeat on the other short end. Repeat this step for the second channel fabric strip.

10 Fold each channel strip in half with the wrong sides together, aligning the long raw edges, and press.

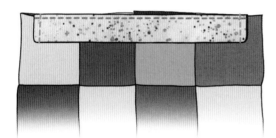

11 Position a folded channel piece on the center of one of one side of the bag, aligning the raw edges. Pin or clip in place and repeat for the second side. Working with the sewing machine's free arm, sew each channel in place within the ¼in (0.5cm) seam allowance, rotating the work around the free arm so you don't sew both layers of the bag together.

12 Working with some lengths of perle cotton, hand-sew some accent cross stitches (see page 124) to each side of the bag.

13 Slide the patchwork panel inside the lining—the right sides will be facing. Align the side seams and the raw edges around the top, and pin or clip in place.

14 Working with the sewing machine's free arm, sew around the top of the bag (see step 9 on page 61 of the E-reader/Tablet Sleeve).

see step 9 on page 61 of the E-reader/Tablet Sleeve

TIP
Cotton webbing tape has been used for the drawstrings, but you can swap these out for thin cord or ribbons to change the look of the drawstring bag.

15 Carefully trim the bulk at the corners (see page 119), being careful not to cut any of the stitches. Working through the gap in the base of the lining, turn the bag and lining to the right side and carefully push out all the corners. Sew up the gap in the base of the lining before pushing the lining inside the bag.

16 Take one length of cotton twill tape and fix a safety pin to the end. Starting at the left-hand side, work the cord through the channel on the front of the bag. Once out of the channel, turn and work the tape through the second channel. This will leave two tails on the left and a loop on the right. Repeat with the second piece of cotton tape, starting from the right-hand side. This will leave two tails on the right-hand side and a loop on the left.

17 The ends can be drawn up to pull the opening of the bag closed. Add cord stops or beads to each side as desired.

Finishing
Trim any excess threads and press lightly to neaten.

e-reader/tablet sleeve

This custom padded sleeve will protect your e-reader or tablet from bumps and scrapes. This sleeve is made using a string block technique and is ideal for using up long thin offcuts of your favorite prints.

FABRIC AND MATERIALS

Cotton fabric scraps in a selection of prints

Cotton foundation fabric

Cotton lining fabric

Fusible foam interlining, Vlieseline Style-Vil Fix, 12½in x 8¼in (32 x 21cm).

Coordinating thread

TOOLS AND EQUIPMENT

Basic quilting kit (see page 6)

FINISHED MEASUREMENTS

8in (20cm) tall x 6in (15cm) wide (fits a Kindle Paperwhite 10th Gen)

CUTTING INSTRUCTIONS

Print cotton fabric scraps: Cut a selection of strips, each 1–2in (2.5–5cm) wide by 8–12in (20–30cm) long

Cotton foundation fabric: Cut two pieces, each 4 x 9in (10 x 22.8cm)

Cotton lining fabric: Cut two pieces, each 6½ x 8½in (16.5 x 21.6cm)

Fusible foam interlining: Cut two pieces, each 6¼ x 8¼in (16 x 21cm)

1 Press the print cotton fabric strips. Ensure that all the strips together will cover the foundation fabric pieces.

2 Place the first fabric strip onto the foundation fabric diagonally across the center with the right side uppermost. Place the next fabric strip on top, with one long edge aligned and the right sides of the fabrics strips together. Pin and then sew in place.

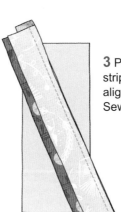

3 Press the strips open. Position the next strip on top with the right sides together, aligning one raw long edge and pin in place. Sew in place.

4 Continue in this manner until the whole foundation fabric is covered. Turn the piece over so the foundation fabric is uppermost. Using a rotary cutter and ruler, trim away the excess fabric around the sides of the foundation fabric. Make three more panels in the same manner, so you have two for the front and two for the back.

5 Pin two of the panels together with the right sides together. Sew along one long edge. Press the seam open. Repeat to join the second pair of panels for the back in the same manner.

6 Place a fusible foam interlining piece onto the wrong side of a patchwork panel, ensuring the adhesive side is facing the wrong side of the panel. Fuse in place with the iron and allow to cool fully. Repeat for the second foam interlining piece and patchwork panel.

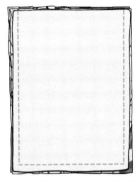

7 Place the panels together with the right sides facing. Sew together, leaving the top short edge unsewn. Trim away the bulk in the seam allowance, including any foam interlining. Clip the lower corners to reduce the bulk (see page 119).

8 Place the two lining pieces together with the right sides facing and pin or clip in place. Sew together, leaving the top short edge unsewn and leaving a 2in (5cm) gap in the seam along the bottom edge. Carefully clip the excess seam allowance at the corners. Turn through, so the right side of the lining fabric is on the outside.

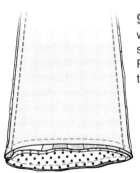

9 Insert the lining into the patchwork piece with the right sides facing. Align the side seams and the raw edges around the top. Pin or clip in place. Sew together around the top, using the sewing machine's free arm.

10 Turn the whole project to the right side through the gap in the bottom of the lining. Push out the corners. Press the seam allowance inward along the gap in the lining and sew the gap closed by hand or machine. Push the lining inside the sleeve to finish.

Finishing
Trim any excess threads and press lightly to neaten.

TIPS
This design has been made using a Kindle Paperwhite, but you can adapt the size to suit your own gadget. Simply ensure that the finished panels and lining are 1in (2.5cm) larger than your device on each side. This will give a snug fit once it is seamed up.

String blocks are great for using up fabric strips. They are sewn onto a foundation fabric, which isn't seen on the finished piece. If you use fabric from your stash for the foundation fabric, just be aware that a dark or printed fabric might show through lighter strips once sewn.

on-the-go project bag

Many quilting projects start out as small pieces. Having a place to stow them means you can pick up your project whenever the mood takes you. The clear vinyl panel allows you to see at a glance what is stored inside.

FABRIC AND MATERIALS

Cotton fabric scraps in a selection of prints (I used gray and green prints)

Medium-loft fusible batting (wadding), Vlieseline H640, 10 x 14in (25.5 x 35.5cm)

Fusible interlining, Vlieseline G700, 10 x 14in (25.5 x 35.5cm)

Cotton backing fabric (inner), 10 x 14in (25.5 x 35.5cm)

Cotton backing fabric (outer), 10 x 14in (25.5 x 35.5cm)

Clear bag-making vinyl, 6 x 10¼in (15 x 26cm)

Coordinating thread

Zipper, 12in (30cm) long

TOOLS AND EQUIPMENT

Basic quilting kit (see page 6)

Zipper foot

Fabric adhesive stick (optional)

Heat- or water-erasable marker

FINISHED MEASUREMENTS

12¼ x 9¼in (31 x 23.5cm)

CUTTING INSTRUCTIONS

Print cotton fabric scraps:

Gray fabric: Cut two 2in (5cm) squares, for the zipper tab

Green fabric: Cut one 2 x 13 (5 x 33cm) piece, for the upper zipper panel

Green fabric: Cut one 1¾ x 13in (4.5 x 33cm) piece, for the lower zipper panel

Green fabric: Cut one 1¾ x 13in (4.5 x 33cm) piece, for the lower panel

Gray fabric: Cut two 2 x 6in (5 x 15cm) pieces, for the side panels

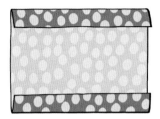

1 Place a zipper tab piece with the wrong side uppermost. Fold each long edge to the wrong side by ¼in (0.5cm) and press.

2 Fold the tab in half, aligning the two folded edges so the raw edges are now concealed. Repeat steps 1 and 2 to make the second zipper tab.

3 Place one tab over a short end of the zipper so it conceals the zipper tape and glue-baste in place. Use a zipper foot to sew the tab in place, being careful not to stitch over the zipper teeth as this can break the needle. Repeat to sew the second tab to the other end of the zipper.

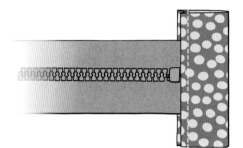

4 Prepare the bag front panels (the upper zipper panel, lower zipper panel, lower panel, and side panels) by using an iron and pressing cloth to fuse the interlining to the wrong side of the fabric. Set aside to cool fully. Cut each piece from the interlining.

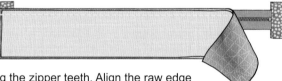

5 With the right side of the zipper facing up, position the upper zipper panel on top with the right side of the fabric facing the zipper teeth. Align the raw edge of the fabric with the raw edge of the zipper tape and pin or clip on place. Using the zipper foot (see tip on page 64), sew close to the zipper teeth to secure the panel to the zipper tape.

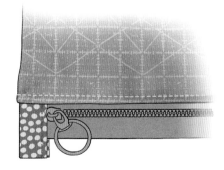

6 Fold the back the panel and press neatly. Topstitch (see page 119) along the edge of the folded panel to secure.

7 Repeat steps 5 and 6 to sew the Lower Zipper Panel to the other side of the zipper tape and then topstitch along the edge of the folded panel. Use a rotary cutter and ruler to square off the long sides of the panels.

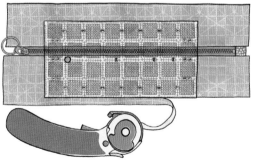

8 Place the inner backing fabric onto the batting with its wrong side facing the fusible side of the batting. Fuse into place with an iron and pressing cloth, and set aside to cool fully.

9 Place the fused batting onto the wrong side of the outer backing fabric. This will create a sandwich of fabric around the batting. Pin or spray baste into place.

TIPS

Clear vinyl is great for bag-making projects. Always cover the vinyl with a pressing cloth before pressing to ensure you don't melt it onto the iron. A non-stick sewing-machine foot (sometimes called a Teflon foot) is ideal for sewing clear vinyl, as it glides over the surface. If you don't have one, place a piece of baking parchment over the vinyl before sewing which you can rip off.

Use fabric clips for clear vinyl, to avoid making holes that will be visible on the finished surface. Also, taking care when sewing as while you can unpick incorrect seams in fabric, the stitch holes in the vinyl will remain visible.

TIP

A zipper foot is a smaller sewing-machine foot that allows you to sew much closer to the edge of the zipper. It can be positioned to sit to the left or right-hand side of the machine's needle so that the stitches run neatly close to the zipper teeth.

10 Working with a walking foot or a free-motion quilting foot, quilt the backing panel as desired. Here the piece has been quilted with a geometric diamond design using a walking foot.

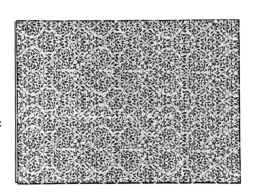

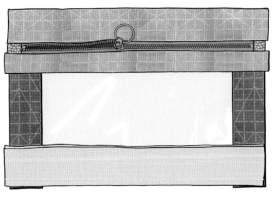

11 Place one of the side panels onto the clear vinyl piece with the right sides facing. Align the raw edges. Clip in place (see tip on page 63). Sew the panel in place, then open it out and press fully using a pressing cloth. Press the seam allowance toward the fabric. Repeat to sew the second side panel to the vinyl.

12 Place the zipper panel onto one long side of the vinyl panel with the right sides facing, and clip in place. Sew in place, then press open using a pressing cloth. Press the seam allowance up toward the fabric. Place the lower panel onto the lower edge of the vinyl with the right sides facing and clip in place. Sew in place and press open.

13 Cover the whole bag front piece with a pressing cloth and press fully. Allow the vinyl to fully cool before moving or touching it.

14 Place the backing panel with the outer fabric uppermost (this will be the fabric that is on the back of the completed bag). Place the bag front on top with its wrong side uppermost. Ensure the zipper is partially open. Clip in place.

15 Sew around all four sides of the bag to join the front and the back panels. As the zipper is left partially open, there is no need to leave a gap in the seam for turning through. Cut away the excess seam allowance at the corners (see page 119).

16 Open the zipper fully and turn the entire bag to the right side through the opening. Push out the corners fully, using a poking tool or knitting needle as needed.

Finishing

Trim any excess threads, cover fully with a pressing cloth, and press lightly to neaten.

tote bag

The diagonal panel gives an interesting twist to these simple patchwork squares. This tote bag is made with a fusible foam interlining, which gives it soft but sturdy finish, ideal for a trip to the bookstore or the farmers' market.

FABRIC AND MATERIALS

Fabric scraps in a selection of prints, totalling approx. 20 x 25in (51 x 63.5cm)

Blue cotton chambray, 15 x 30in (38 x 76.2cm)

Cream cotton, 25in x 30in (63.5 x 76.2cm)

Fusible foam interlining, Vlieseline Style-Vil Fix, 16 x 30in (40.5 x 76cm)

Cotton webbing, 100in (254cm)

Coordinating thread

TOOLS AND EQUIPMENT

Basic sewing kit (see page 6)

Hand-sewing needle

FINISHED MEASUREMENTS

10½in (26.5cm) wide, 12½in (32cm) tall, 4in (10cm) deep

TIP

The squares for the panel have been rotated to create a diagonal design. While this looks more complex, the principle is the same. The squares are worked into rows and which are then joined together to create the panel. To avoid any confusion, you can make small paper tags to pin to each square or row to help you join them in the right order.

CUTTING INSTRUCTIONS

Print cotton fabric scraps: Cut forty-six 2in (5cm) squares, for the panel

Blue cotton chambray: Cut two 6 x 15in (15 x 38cm) pieces, for the Lower Panel

Cream cotton: Cut two 21 x 15in (53.4 x 38cm) pieces, for the Upper Panel (this includes the lining)

Cotton webbing: Cut two 50in (127cm) pieces, for the straps

Fusible foam interlining: Cut two 16 x 15in (40.5 x 38cm) pieces. Along one short lower edge of each piece, cut a 2in (5cm) square from each corner.

1 Arrange the small squares to create the diagonal squares panel until you are happy with the arrangement. Follow steps 2–4 on page 121 to join the squares in each diagonal row, working with pairs of squares at a time. Follow steps 5–7 on page 121 to join the rows together. Press all the seam allowances in the same direction. Repeat to make a second panel in the same manner.

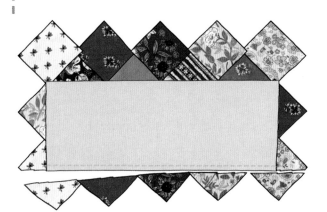

2 Place a Lower Panel onto the lower edge of one of the diagonal panels with the right sides facing. Ensure the diagonal panel is covered by the width of the Lower Panel— some portions of the diagonal squares will extend beyond the edges. Sew in place. Using a rotary cutter and ruler, trim away the excess squares from the lower edge.

3 Place one of the Upper Panels onto the upper edge of a diagonal panel in the same manner as step 2 and pin in place. Sew together, and use a rotary cutter and ruler to trim away the excess. Press the panel open fully, pressing the seam allowances toward the diagonal panel. Cut a 2in (5cm) square from each corner of the panel. Repeat steps 2 and 3 to make the second panel in the same manner.

TIP

The fusible foam interlining (Vlieseline Style-Vil Fix) gives this bag a soft, structured finish. It is a voluminous, dense foam that gives a padded finish to the bag. It is also ideal for making glasses cases and phone covers. While it can be very easily sewn by both hand and machine, you may prefer to use a walking foot when sewing it, as this will help the thick layers feed more evenly through the sewing machine.

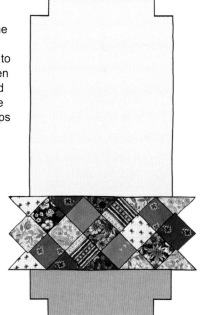

4 Place the foam interlining with the fusible side uppermost. Place the lower portion of the bag, with its right side uppermost, on top of the foam interlining, matching up the corners. Cover with a pressing cloth and fuse in place. Allow to cool fully and repeat for the second side of the bag.

5 Take one length of cotton webbing and position its raw edges along the lower edge of the bag. Ensure that each end of the webbing is at least 2in (5cm) from the corner and that the strap isn't twisted. Pin in place. Working with in the ¼in (0.5cm) seam allowance, sew the strap ends to the base of the bag. Then work a line of discreet hand stitching or use fabric glue to secure the straps to the bag, but don't go beyond the top of the patchwork panel. Repeat to secure the second webbing piece to the other bag panel.

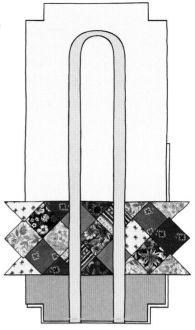

6 Fold the straps out of the way of the edge of the panels, and pin in place in preparation for sewing the seams.

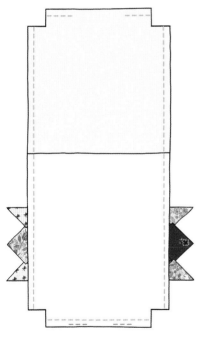

7 Place the two sides of the bag together with the right sides facing. Align the lower sections of the foam interlining and clip in place. Align the side seams and raw the edges of the cotton and pin or clip in place. Working with a walking foot as needed, sew along the bottom of the bag between the two cut sections at the corners. Stitch up each long side in turn. Sew along top edge between the cut corners, leaving a 4in (10cm) gap.

8 Sew the boxed corners in the base of the bag by opening out each cut square and aligning the side seams at the top and bottom (see step 6 on page 76). Align the raw edges and clip in place, then sew along the straight edge. Repeat to sew the boxed corners in the lining.

9 Carefully turn the whole bag to the right side through the gap in the lining. Push the boxed corners out fully. The lining section will extend above the upper section of the bag.

10 Push the lining the inside the bag. Position and pin the straps into place at the top of the bag. Topstitch (see page 119) around the top of the bag, ¼in (0.5cm) from the edge, to fix the straps into position.

Finishing
Trim any excess threads and press lightly to neaten.

belt bag

Stow your essentials in style with this belted bag, which is perfect for a trip to the gym or a summer festival. This design is made with a simple quilted panel and a zipper fastening and features an adjustable strap for a custom fit.

FABRIC AND MATERIALS

Cotton fabric scraps in a selection of prints, each with a maximum size of 9 x 22in (23 x 56cm), or Fat Eighths in eight different prints

Cotton lining fabric, 11 x 12in (28 x 30cm)

Fusible woven interlining, Vlieseline G700, 3 x 10in (7.5 x 25.5cm)

Batting (wadding), 11 x 12in (28 x 30cm)

10in (25.5cm) zipper

Coordinating thread

Bag buckle and strap adjuster, each 1¼in (3cm) wide

Cotton webbing, 42in (106cm)

TOOLS AND EQUIPMENT

Basic sewing kit (see page 6)

Zipper foot

Spray adhesive (optional)

Fabric glue stick (optional)

TEMPLATE (SEE PAGE 126)

Belt bag strap end

FINISHED MEASUREMENTS

15in (38cm) long (including strap tabs) x 5in (13cm) deep

CUTTING INSTRUCTIONS

Print cotton fabric scraps or Fat Eighths:

Cut one 5¾ x 2in (14.6 x 5cm) piece in fabric A

Cut one 5¾ x 4in (14.6 x 10cm) piece in fabric B

Cut one 5¾ x 2½in (14.6 x 6.5cm) piece in fabric C

Cut one 5¾ x 4¾in (14.6 x 12cm) piece in fabric D

Cut one 12¼ x 1¾in (31 x 4.5cm) piece in fabric E

Cut one 4¼ x 4in (10.8 x 10cm) piece in fabric F

Cut one 8 x 4in (20 x 10cm) piece in fabric G

Cut two 2 x 3in (5 x 7.5cm) pieces, for the tabs

Cut four pieces using the template, for the bag strap tabs

Fusible woven interlining: Cut four pieces using the template, for the bag strap tabs

Cotton webbing: Cut one 30in (76cm) length and one 12in (30cm) length

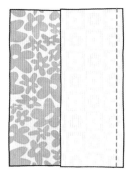

1 Place pieces A and B together with their right sides facing, aligning their long sides. Pin or clip in place and sew together. Press the fabric open, pressing the seam allowance open (see page 119).

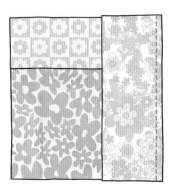

2 Place piece C on top of the work, on one of the sides of the joined pieces, aligning the raw edges. Pin or clip in place and sew together. Press the fabric open, pressing the seam allowance open.

3 Place piece D on top of the work on the opposite side of the joined pieces, aligning the raw edges. Pin or clip in place and sew together. Press the fabric open, pressing the seam allowance open.

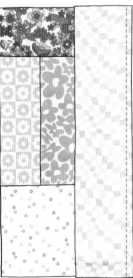

4 Place piece E on top of the work, along the top long side, aligning the raw edges. Pin or clip in place and sew together. Press the fabric open, pressing the seam allowance open.

5 Place pieces F and G together with their right sides facing, aligning their short ends. Pin or clip in place and sew together. Press the fabrics open, pressing the seams open.

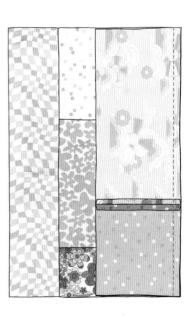

6 Place the joined F-and-G strip onto the work along the long lower edge with the right sides facing. Align the raw edges and pin or clip pin place. Sew together, then press the fabric open, pressing the seam allowance open.

7 Spray a small amount of adhesive onto the batting, then place the panel on top with its right side uppermost. Press the panel to baste it in place. Quilt the panel using your preferred method. Here the panel has been free-motion quilted using a wavy stitch motif (see tip).

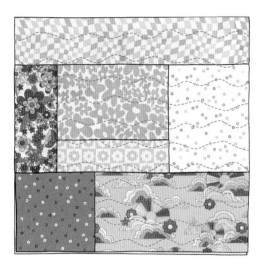

TIPS

This panel is quilted with free-motion wavy lines. Free motion sewing is done by removing the feed dogs and working with a free-motion foot, gently guiding the fabric through the machine to place the stitches. The panel can also be quilted by hand or by using straight-line quilting motifs.

A zipper foot is a useful attachment for a sewing machine. It reduces the pressure from the feed dogs, allowing the fabric and webbing to feed through the machine more easily. It also can be moved either side of the needle to allow you to position the stitching close to the zipper for a neat finish.

8 Follow steps 1–3 on page 62 of the On-the-go Project Bag to make the zipper tabs and sew them to either end of the zipper.

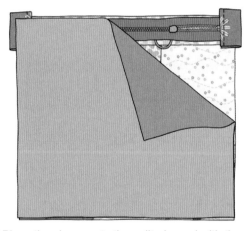

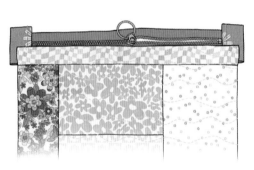

9 Place the zipper onto the quilted panel with the zipper teeth facing the right side of the panel. Place the lining fabric on top with the right sides facing. The zipper is sandwiched between the quilted panel and the lining. Glue-baste the zipper in place or pin or clip it in place. Using a zipper foot, sew along the top of the work to secure the zipper in between the panel and the lining, ensuring that the stitches are close to the teeth.

10 Fold back the panel and the lining to reveal the secured zipper. The wrong sides of the lining and the panel will be facing. Press to neaten.

11 Follow step 8 on page 54 of the Scrappy Boxy Pouch to fold back the panel so its long raw edge is aligned with the unstitched side of the zipper tape. Fold over the lining so that its long raw edge is aligned with the unstitched side of the zipper tape. The zip is sandwiched between the lining and the quilted panel. Glue-baste in place or pin or clip in place.

12 With a zipper foot, sew along the long raw edge to secure the zipper in between the panel and the lining, as you did in step 9, ensuring that the stitches are close to the teeth. Turn the work through so that the quilted panel is innermost and the lining is outermost. Position the zipper so that it lies 1in (2.5cm) from the folded edge at the top of the bag. Press fully.

13 Place an interlining piece onto the wrong side of each of the bag strap tab pieces and fuse into place. Allow to cool fully.

14 Feed the 12in (30cm) piece of cotton webbing through the "insertion" part of the buckle and align the raw edges.

15 With a bag tab piece right side up, place the cotton webbing on top, so the webbing extends slightly over the short ends of the tab.

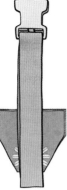

16 Place the second bag tab piece on top with the right sides facing and pin in place. Sew around the edge of the tab to secure the webbing in place, leaving the wide end of the tab unstitched.

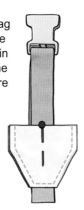

17 Clip into the seam allowance to reduce the bulk at the corners (see page 119). Turn the tab through to the right side and press fully. Set aside.

18 Feed the remaining 30in (76cm) length of cotton webbing through the strap adjuster, then feed it through the pronged part of the buckle.

19 Turn the strap over and feed the end of the webbing back through the strap adjuster.

20 Tuck the raw edge under by 1¼in (3cm) and pin in place. Sew to secure the fold by working a rectangle of stitching over the fold. Sew diagonally through the shape to form a cross to reinforce it.

21 Follow steps 15–17 to sew the second two bag strap tabs to the raw end of the webbing.

22 With the bag partly unzipped and lining outermost, position the straps inside the bag, sandwiching the ends of the strap tabs in each of the side seams. Be sure that the straps are the in the correct orientation and not twisted, and pin or clip in place. Use a plate or bowl to draw a curve at the two lower corners of the bag. Sew each side seam, following the curve at the bottom. Use pinking shears to clip the bulk along the curved lower seams. Turn the bag through to the right side and press fully.

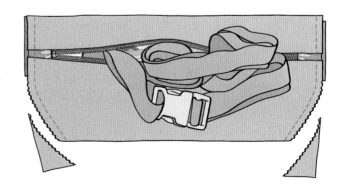

Finishing
Trim any excess threads and press lightly to neaten.

chapter 3
home & wall décor

plant pot tub and mat

Enter your houseplant era with this patchwork combo. Made with simple squares of fabric, this patchwork bucket and mat are great additions to your interiors and would be wonderful housewarming gifts, too.

FABRIC AND MATERIALS

Cotton fabric scraps in a selection of prints

Outer main fabric, 15 x 25in (38 x 63.5cm), for the tub and mat

Lining fabric, 16 x 9in (40.6 x 23cm), for the tub

Fusible interlining, 16 x 9in (40.6 x 23cm), for the tub

Backing fabric, 7in (18cm) square, for the mat

Batting (wadding), 7in (18cm) square, for the mat

Coordinating thread

TOOLS AND EQUIPMENT

Basic quilting kit (see page 6)

Air-erasable or water-soluble marker

Spray adhesive (optional)

Hand-sewing needle

FINISHED MEASUREMENTS

Pot tub: 6in (15cm) wide x 3½in (9cm) deep x 5½in (14cm) tall

Mat: 6in (15cm) square

CUTTING INSTRUCTIONS

FOR THE POT TUB:

Print cotton fabric scraps: Cut twenty 2¼in (5.8cm) squares

Outer main fabric: Cut two 4¾ x 8in (12 x 20cm) pieces

Lining fabric: Cut two 8 x 9in (20 x 23cm) pieces

Fusible interlining: Cut two 8 x 9in (20 x 23cm) pieces

FOR THE MAT:

Print cotton fabric scraps: Cut six 2¼in (5.8cm) squares

Outer main fabric: Cut one 2¼in x 6½in (5.8 x 16.5cm) piece

plant pot tub

1 Lay out the 2¼in (5.8cm) squares into two rows of five squares, and arrange until you're happy with the placement. Start with one of the rows. Working with two adjacent squares in turn and placing them together with the right sides facing, follow steps 2–4 on page 121 to join the squares to make two rows and press the seams in alternate directions.

2 Follow step 5 on page 121 to join the rows together, neatly nesting (see page 120) the seam allowances. Press fully and repeat steps 1 and 2 to create a second patchwork piece.

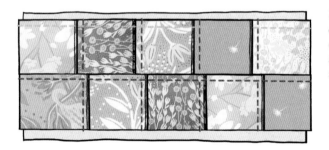

3 With the right sides facing, place one patchwork panel onto an outer main fabric piece, aligning the long raw edges. Pin or clip in place and sew together. Press fully and repeat to sew the second patchwork panel onto the second main outer fabric piece.

4 Press one of the patchwork panels away from the main outer piece. With a rotary cutter, ruler, and cutting mat, trim away any excess fabric from the patchwork panel along each side. Repeat for the second patchwork panel.

TIP
Both the pot tub and the mat require turning through, so be sure to leave a gap in the seam to turn each one though—usually 2–3in (5–7.5cm) is plenty. Work reverse stitches at the start and end of the seam either side of the gap to give additional strength to the stitches when turning though. Work slowly when you're turning each piece through to the right side, pushing out all corners and curves before pressing.

5 Place the two panels right sides together and pin or clip along the sides and base. Using the ruler and air-erasable or water-soluble marker, mark out a 1½in (4cm) square at each of the two lower corners of the main fabric. Carefully cut these out. Sew the two side seams and the base seam (working between the two cut corners). Press fully.

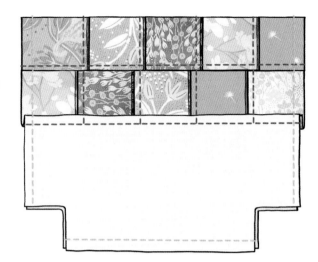

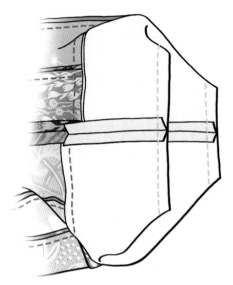

6 Open out the tub and align the seams at one side and along the base. Align the edges along one of the squares you cut at a corner. The cut edge will form a neat line across the corner. Pin or clip in place. Sew the corner seam, taking a ¼in (0.5cm) seam allowance from the raw edge. Repeat on the other side to create the boxed corners.

7 Place one of the fusible interlining pieces onto the wrong side of one of the lining pieces and fuse in place. Allow to cool fully. Repeat with the second interlining piece and second lining piece.

8 Place the two interfaced lining sections together with the right sides facing and pin or clip in place. Follow step 5 to cut a square at each of the lower corners, and sew the two side seams and the base seam. Press fully.

9 Follow step 6 to sew the two boxed-corner seams.

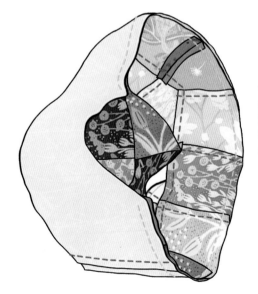

10 With the right sides of the patchwork piece outermost, place it inside the lining bag so right sides of the fabrics are facing. Align the side seams and the raw edges around the top. Pin or clip in place. Sew around the top edge, leaving a 2–3in (5–7.5cm) gap in the seam for turning through.

11 Turn the pot tub to the right side through the gap in the seam. Push the lining inside the outer tub and press. Using ladder stitch (see page 124), sew the gap in the seam closed.

plant pot mat

1 Lay out the 2¼in (5.8cm) squares into two rows of three squares, and arrange them until you are happy with the placement. Take the first square in each row and place them together with the right sides facing and pin or clip in place. Sew together (see page 121). Repeat to sew the second squares in each row together, and then the third squares—you can chain piece here if desired (see page 123). Press the seams in alternating directions (see page 121). Place two pairs of squares together with the right sides facing and the seams nested (see page 120) and pin or clip in place. Sew the two pairs together. Repeat to join the remaining piece.

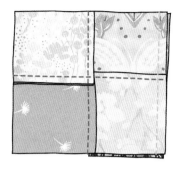

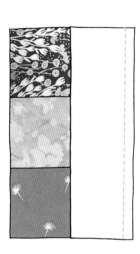

2 Open out the panel and press it fully. Place the main fabric strip onto the patchwork panel with the right sides facing. Align the raw edges, pin or clip in place, and sew together.

3 Open out the panel and press. Place the panel onto the batting, leaving a 1in (2.5cm) border around each side. Pin or spray-baste the panel into place. Quilt as desired—this piece has been machine quilted using straight-line stitching following the lines of the patchwork.

4 Using a rotary cutter, ruler and mat, trim the excess batting so the block is square. Place the backing fabric on top of the quilted panel with the right sides facing and pin or clip in place. Using an air-erasable or water-soluble marker, draw around the base of a cotton reel or egg cup to mark an even curve at each corner. Sew around the raw edges, following the curved guides at the corners. Leave a small gap in the seam for turning through.

5 Make small clips into the seam allowance around the curves to reduce the bulk (see page 119). Be sure not to snip through the stitching.

6 Carefully turn the mat to the right side through the gap in the seam. Tuck in the seam allowance along the gap and press. Hand-sew the gap closed using ladder stitch.

Finishing
Trim any excess threads and press lightly to neaten.

heart talk wall hanging

This bold statement mini quilt is sure to get people talking. The heart motif is worked in a mosaic pixel style using simple squares and half-square triangles. The finished quilted panel is trimmed down to a stylized speech bubble design to give the wall hanging maximum impact.

FABRIC AND MATERIALS

Cotton fabric scraps in a selection of prints—pink and low volume

Quilter's Grid or lightweight fusible interlining (see tip)

Cotton backing fabric

Binding, 40in (102cm)

Batting (wadding), 15in x 20in (38 x 51cm)

Coordinating thread

Wooden doweling, 14in (35.5cm)

TOOLS AND EQUIPMENT

Basic quilting kit (see page 6)

Spray adhesive (optional)

Hand-sewing needle

CHART AND TEMPLATE (SEE PAGE 126)

Heart talk placement chart

Heart talk speech bubble template

FINISHED MEASUREMENTS

Approx. 12 x 17in (30 x 43cm)

1 Place a pink and a low-volume 2½in (6.5cm) square together with the right sides facing and follow steps 1–3 on page 122 to make two Half Square Triangles (HST). Repeat to create ten pink-and-low-volume HST in total. Then repeat to create a further 33 low-volume HST. These can be chain-pieced if you prefer (see page 123).

follow steps 1–3 on page 122; see page 123; following the chart on page 126

CUTTING INSTRUCTIONS

Cotton fabric scraps:

Cut five pink 2½in (6.5cm) squares, for the Half Square Triangles

Cut thirty-three low-volume 2½in (6.5cm) squares, for the background Half Square Triangles

Cut twenty pink 2in (5cm) squares

Cut thirty-four low-volume 2in (5cm) squares, for the background

Cut two 2½ x 4in (6.5 x 10cm) pieces, for the hanging sleeves

Quilter's Grid or interlining: Cut four 8 x 12in (20 x 30cm) pieces

2 The four pieces of Quilter's Grid or interlining will make up a quarter of the quilt each. Each quarter is worked in turn before they are joined together. With the fusible side uppermost and following the chart on page 126, place the HST and fabric squares into place using the grid lines to make four rows of six squares on each piece of the Quilter's Grid or interlining. Cover with a pressing cloth and carefully fuse the squares in place. Be careful not to fuse the interlining to the pressing cloth—you can trim away the excess before fusing if you prefer.

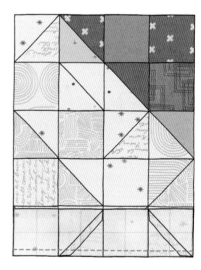

3 Once the interlining has cooled and the fabrics are fully bonded, take one of the quarters of the quilt. Fold the fabric with the right sides together along the line where the two of the four-square rows meet—on the Quilter's Grid there is a printed line to follow. Sew along the fold ¼in (0.5cm) from the folded edge—this creates the ¼in (0.5cm) seam allowance.

TIP

This heart pixel design is created using Quilter's Grid, which is a pre-printed interlining ideal for working perfectly neat seams and creating a mosaic design. Here the fabrics are placed in line with the grid, fused on, and then folded and stitched on the wrong side to create the seams. This fuse, fold, and stitch technique can also be achieved using lightweight fusible interlining, ideally working with a cutting mat underneath to ensure precise placement of the squares.

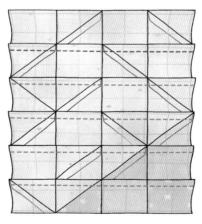

4 Repeat step 3 to sew all the of the seams joining the four-square rows.

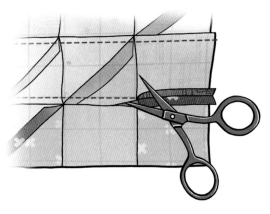

5 Use a pair of small sharp scissors to carefully cut along the fold of each seam allowance. Press the seams open (see page 119).

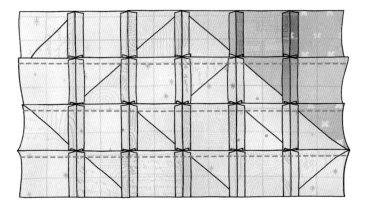

6 Using the same method as step 3, fold and sew along the lines where the six-square rows meet, ensuring the seam allowances you pressed in the previous step are folded open. Then follow step 5 to cut along the fold of each seam allowance. Make sure all the seams on the panel are pressed open.

7 Repeat steps 2–6 to sew the three remaining panels of the quilt.

8 Place the two lower panels together along their short sides with their right sides facing. Make sure the raw edges are aligned. Pin or clip in place, then sew together. Join the upper panels together in the same manner. Press the panels fully.

9 Place the two sections together along their long edges with the right sides facing. Make sure the raw edges are aligned. Pin or clip in place, then sew together.

10 Place the backing fabric with the wrong side uppermost and then position the batting on top. Apply a small amount of spray adhesive to the batting, then place the quilt top with its right side uppermost on the batting, leaving a border of batting around the quilt top. Press the quilt top onto the batting to fix it in place.

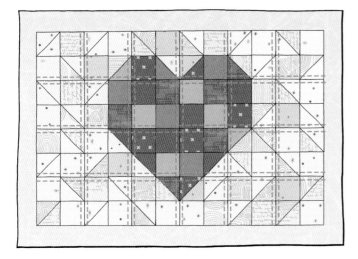

11 Machine-quilt as desired. Here straight lines have been sewn following the fabric squares to create a grid motif.

12 Place the speech bubble template onto the quilt top, ensuring that you are happy with the placement. Pin in place and cut around the template.

13 Follow the steps on page 123 to attach the binding around the edge of the quilt.

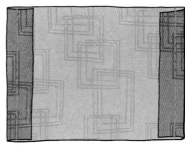

14 Fold the short ends of each of the hanging sleeve strips to the wrong side by ½in (1.3cm). Pin or clip, and then sew each fold in place.

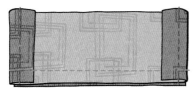

15 Fold the strip with its right sides facing, aligning the two long raw edges. Pin or clip in place. Sew along the long raw edges. Repeat steps 14–15 to make a second hanging sleeve. Turn each sleeve through to the right side.

16 Place the two hanging sleeves near the top of the wrong side of the quilt, positioning them parallel to the horizontal stitch lines, and pin in place. Hand-sew each sleeve into place with ladder stitch (see page 124) along the long sides of each sleeve.

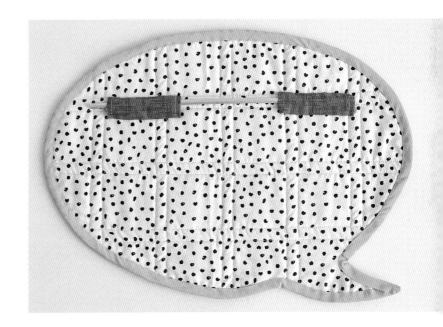

Making up and finishing
Trim any excess threads and press lightly to neaten. Slide the piece of doweling into the hanging sleeves to finish.

TIP
This quilt features hanging sleeves at the back of the work that allow you to insert a small dowel rod. The rod can be hung on a regular picture hook or nail, giving the effect of the quilt floating on the wall.

somerset hanging star

Despite looking incredibly intricate, this design is created by the careful folding and placement of pretty fabric squares. The motif is also known as the Folded Star, can be worked in any fabrics, and looks fabulous in festive prints for a seasonal decoration.

FABRIC AND MATERIALS

Scraps in a selection of prints:

Fabric A (center): 8in (20cm) square

Fabric B (Star 1): 20in (51cm) square

Fabric C (Star 2): 20in (51cm) square

Fabric D (Star 3): 20in (51cm) square

Fabric E (Star 4): 20in (51cm) square

White cotton foundation fabric (not seen on the finished piece) 13in (33cm) square

Felt for backing hoop, 12in (30cm) square

Cotton twill tape ribbon, 12in (30cm) long

Embroidery hoop, 9in (23cm) diameter

Coordinating thread

TOOLS AND EQUIPMENT

Basic quilting kit (see page 6)

Air-erase or water-soluble marker (test on a fabric scrap before using on project)

Wooden clapper or block (optional, see tip)

FINISHED MEASUREMENTS

9in (23cm) diameter, excluding twill loop

CUTTING INSTRUCTIONS

Fabric A: Cut four 4in (10cm) squares

Fabric B: Cut eight 5in (12.7cm) squares

Fabric C: Cut eight 5in (12.7cm) squares

Fabric D: Cut eight 5in (12.7cm) squares

Fabric E: Cut eight 5in (12.7cm) squares

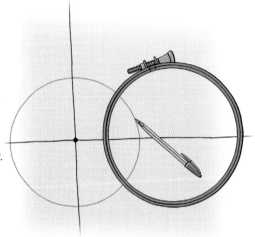

1 Place the embroidery hoop into the center of the foundation fabric and draw around the inside of the hoop. Fold the circle in half and then half again, and mark the center point with a water-soluble or air-erasable marker.

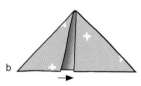

2 Press one of the fabric squares with its wrong side uppermost. Fold it in half from the top to the lower edge, aligning the raw edges. Press neatly. The right side of the fabric is now uppermost. Take each upper corner in turn and fold along the dotted line toward the center of the bottom edge (a). This will create a point in the center at the top (b). Press in place. Repeat to fold the rest of the fabric squares.

TIP
This project uses a sewing machine to secure the pieces, but if you wish you can hand-sew the elements into place, making this a portable project that you can sew on the go!

3 Place the first folded Fabric A piece onto the foundation fabric, using the creases in the foundation fabric as guides for where to position the two short sides of the triangle. Pin in place. Repeat to secure all four of the Fabric A pieces in place.

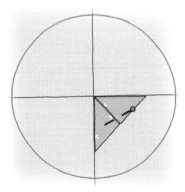

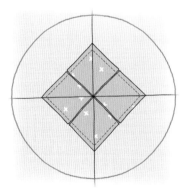

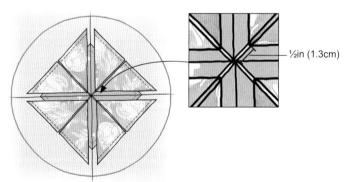

½in (1.3cm)

4 Sew along the outer edge of the folded pieces to secure them to the foundation fabric.

5 Take the eight folded Fabric B pieces for Star 1. Place the first four pieces onto the center element. Use a ruler to ensure each of the points is placed ½in (1.3cm) away from the center point and pin into place. Sew along the outer edge of each of the Fabric B pieces.

6 Place the remaining four Fabric B pieces onto the work, aligning the tips with the folded edges of the center block. Again ensure that the tips of the triangles are positioned ½in (1.3cm) down from the center point and pin in place. Sew along the outer edge of each of the Fabric B pieces.

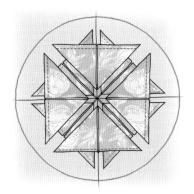

TIP
When pressing the pieces, you may find that pressing and then placing the pieces under a wooden clapper or block will help to secure the neat crip folds. You can also use quilt clips to hold the folds in place—this is particularly handy if you are pressing all the pieces ahead of sewing as it will keep them neat until you are ready to stitch them.

7 Take the eight folded Fabric C pieces for Star 2. Place the first four pieces onto the center element. Use a ruler to check that each of the points is ½in (1.3cm) away from the points on Star 1 and pin into place. Sew along the outer edge of each of the Fabric C pieces. Repeat to pin and sew the remaining four folded Fabric C pieces in position, again ensuring that the tips of the fabric are ½in (1.3cm) away from the points on Star 1.

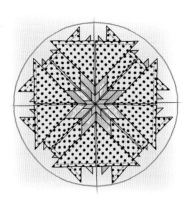

8 Working in the same manner, pin and sew on Stars 3 and 4, following step 7 and working with four elements at a time.

Making up and finishing

Trim any excess threads. Cover with a pressing cloth and neatly press the whole motif, ensuring that all of the points of the star are lying flat.

Draw around the outer edge of the embroidery hoop onto the piece of felt and trim the felt to size.

Separate the two rings of the embroidery hoop. Place the motif onto the smaller ring so it is centered. Place the large ring over the top and push it down, sandwiching the fabric in between to hold it taut. Tighten the screw of the hoop.

Trim the foundation fabric to leave a 1–2in (2.5–5cm) border around the edge. Sew around the fabric bordering the hoop with two rows of gather stitches (see page 124). Draw up to pull the excess fabric into the center and secure.

Place the felt circle onto the back of the hoop to conceal the back of the work and secure it in place with fabric glue.

Fold the length of cotton twill tape in half and knot the short ends together. Secure as a hanging loop under the fastening of the embroidery hoop to finish.

patchwork lampshade

Work with your favorite fabric offcuts to make your own custom interior accent. This patchwork design is made with lightweight cottons and is carefully secured onto a lampshade frame.

FABRIC AND MATERIALS

Lightweight cotton fabric in three different prints, Fat Eighths (see page 5)

Non-woven medium-weight fusible interlining, Vlieseline H250, 7 x 19in (17.8 x 48.3cm)

Coordinating thread

TOOLS AND EQUIPMENT

Basic quilting kit (see page 6)

Lampshade frame, 6in (15cm) diameter

Adhesive lampshade vinyl, 7 x 19in (17.8 x 48.3cm)

Double-sided tape

Seam roller

Hera or crease marker

FINISHED MEASUREMENTS

6in (15cm) tall, approx. 19in (48.3cm) circumference

CUTTING INSTRUCTIONS

Fabric A (multicolored print):
Cut three 3 x 4½in (7.5 x 11.5cm) pieces

Fabric B (pink print):
Cut two 4½ x 5in (11.5 x 12.7cm) pieces

Fabric C (green print):
Cut two 4½ x 5in (11.5 x 12.7cm) pieces

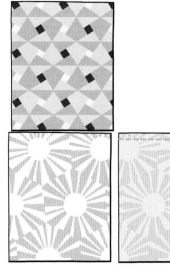

1 Arrange the fabrics to create your chosen design, using the arrangement in step 2 as a guide. Place a Fabric B and Fabric C piece together with the right sides facing and the short edges aligned. Pin or clip in place and sew together (see page 121). Trim the seams to ⅛in (3mm) (see tip below) and press open (see page 119). Repeat to join the second pair of fabric B and fabric C pieces.

2 Arrange the fabrics in your chosen order—here the patchwork squares are placed between the fabric A strips.

TIP

When piecing the patchwork pieces together, use a rotary cutter and ruler to carefully trim back the seam allowance to a scant ⅛in (3mm) and press open. Be very careful not to slice through the stitching. This will help to reduce the bulk around the seams and create a smooth finish.

3 Place the first two pieces in the row together with the right sides facing, aligning the long edges, and pin or clip in place. Sew along one long side. Trim the seam allowance to ⅛in (3mm) and press open. Repeat until all the pieces have been joined to make a row.

4 Place the panel onto the fusible non-woven interlining, with the adhesive side of the interlining facing the wrong side of the patchwork panel. Cover with a pressing cloth and fuse into place. The interlining will cover the seams and give the panel a bit of structure. Leave to cool.

5 Remove the backing from the lampshade vinyl and secure it onto the wrong side of the fabric panel, working slowly to avoid any ripples. The vinyl should be smaller than the fabric, so make sure the border is even on each short side and each long side. Once the vinyl is secured, press firmly or use a seam roller or brayer to ensure that it is smoothly adhered to the fabric. Place a piece of double-sided tape onto one short end of the panel. Leave the backing paper or carrier sheet on the tape for now.

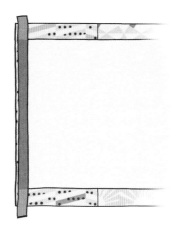

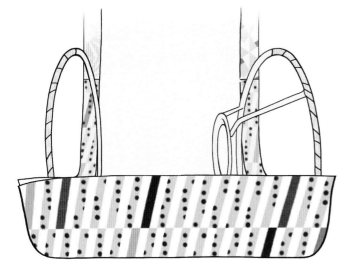

6 Stick a piece of double-sided tape around the outer circle of each section of the lampshade frame. Leave the backing paper or carrier tape in place. Place the patchwork panel with its wrong side uppermost. Starting at the short end without the double-sided tape, position a lampshade frame piece at each side of the panel. Remove the backing paper from the double-sided tape on the lampshade frames. Begin slowing and evenly rolling the frames to secure the panel to the frames. Work slowly to ensure the frames are even and parallel.

7 Once the whole frame has been wrapped, remove the backing paper or carrier from the piece of double-sided tape at the end of the panel and press into position to create the back seam. Use a seam roller to firmly press it into place.

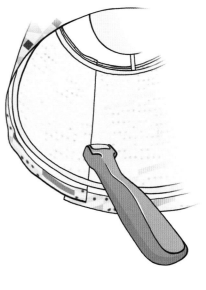

8 Working around the bottom and then the top of the lampshade in turn, fold the excess patchwork fabric over the frame. Press firmly to secure the fabric to the tape on the frame. You can use a Hera or crease tool to help press the fabric in place.

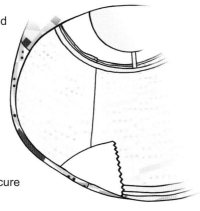

Making up and finishing

Trim any excess threads and secure the lampshade to a light fitting.

TIP

Lampshade hardware can often be found in craft stores or online at specialist retailers. You can buy the elements either separately or in an easy-use kit.

play mat/stroller quilt

Alternating solid squares and four-block squares creates this simple but
fun checkerboard design. This beginner-friendly design makes the most
of lively prints and solid colors. It makes a wonderful play mat and is also
great for keeping small children cozy while out and about in their stroller.

FABRIC AND MATERIALS

Cotton fabrics in a minimum of 6 prints, each measuring 9 x 22in (23 x 56cm) or use Fat Eighths (see page 5)

Cream cotton fabric, 24in (61cm) square

Green cotton fabric, 16 x 24in (40.6 x 61cm)

Cotton backing fabric 35 x 40in (90 x 101.5cm)

Binding,130in (330cm) long

Batting (wadding) 35 x 40in (90 x 101.5cm)

Coordinating thread

TOOLS AND EQUIPMENT

Basic quilting kit (see page 6)

Quilting safety pins (curved)

Quilt basting (tacking) thread and needle

FINISHED MEASUREMENTS

29¼ x 34½in (74 x 87.5cm)

CUTTING INSTRUCTIONS

Print cotton fabrics: Cut sixty 3½in (9cm) squares

Cream cotton: Cut nine 6½in (16.5cm) squares

Green cotton: Cut six 6½in (16.5cm) squares

1 Arrange four of the small 3½in (9cm) squares into two rows of two squares until you are happy with the arrangement.

2 Place together the top pair of squares with the right sides facing and the raw edges aligned and clip or pin into place. Sew together and press the seam allowance to the left-hand side. Repeat to sew the lower pair of squares together, but press the seam allowance to the right-hand side.

3 Place the two seamed pieces together with the right sides facing. Align the raw edges and neatly nest the seams (see page 120). Pin or clip in place, then sew together. Press the block open and press the seam allowance to one side. Use a rotary cutter, ruler, and cutting mat to trim it to a 6½in (16.5cm) square. Repeat to make 14 more blocks, so you have 15 four-square blocks in total.

TIPS

This design is worked using a combination of solid squares and print cotton blocks. You can make it larger by simply repeating the pattern of solid and print blocks. Remember to increase your fabric amounts.

While this quilt is designed as a stroller-friendly size rectangle or play mat and uses natural cotton fibers, babies and small children should always be supervised while using blankets and quilts.

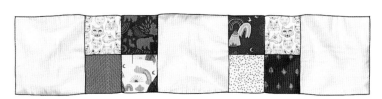

4 Use the photo opposite to arrange the quilt top design, alternating between large plain squares and the four-square print-cotton blocks. Place the first two pieces of the first row together with the right sides facing and align the raw edges. Pin or clip in place, then sew together. Repeat to sew the next square to the row. Continue in the same manner until the row of five blocks is complete. Press fully, pressing the seam allowances all in the same direction.

5 Repeat step 4 to make five more rows in the same manner, so you have six rows of five blocks in total. Press the seam allowances on each row in alternate directions (see page 121).

6 Place the first two rows together with the right sides facing and align the raw edges. Ensure that the seam allowances are neatly nested. Pin or clip in place, then sew the two rows together (see page 121). Press the seam allowances in one direction and repeat to join the remaining rows for the quilt top in the same manner.

7 Press the quilt top and backing fabric fully. Place the backing fabric with its wrong side uppermost and position the batting on top. Smooth out any wrinkles. Layer the quilt top on top with the right side uppermost, leaving a border of about 4in (10cm) of the batting and backing fabric around the quilt top on all sides. Baste (tack) the layers together using your preferred method of pins or basting stitches (see tip).

8 Quilt the project as desired—here the stitch in the ditch method (see page 119) has been used along the edge of each four-square block and large square, giving it a discreet finish.

9 Using a rotary cutter, ruler, and cutting mat, carefully trim away the excess batting and backing fabric from around the quilt top and neatly square up the sides as needed.

10 Follow the steps on page 123 to attach the binding around the outer edge of the quilt.

Finishing
Trim any excess threads and press lightly to neaten.

TIP
While spray adhesive is great for small projects, larger quilts will often need to be basted using either pins or basting (tacking) stitches to hold the layers together for quilting. Use curved safety pins, as these are angled in a way to work through all three layers (the quilt top, batting, and backing) without disrupting the placement. Basting stitches are essentially long, straight running stitches (see page 124) worked through all the layers that can be smoothly removed after the quilting has been worked. Use a contrast color thread to make the removal process easier. Whether working with pins or basting stitches, start at the center and work outward, smoothing out any wrinkles as you go.

table runner

This table runner is made using a disappearing nine block, which despite its intricate appearance is quick and easy to make. Worked with an easy-care, heat-protecting polyester batting, this table runner is suitable for both decoration and everyday use.

FABRIC AND MATERIALS

Cotton fabric scraps in a selection of prints

Cream cotton fabric, 37 x 52in (94 x 132cm), for the backing and border

Binding, 148in (376cm)

Low-loft polyester batting (wadding), Vlieseline Thermolam, 37 x 52in (94 x 132cm)—use two pieces for more heat protection (see tip on page 96)

Coordinating thread

TOOLS AND EQUIPMENT

Basic sewing kit (see page 6)

Spray adhesive (optional)

FINISHED MEASUREMENTS

20½ x 48¼in (52 x 122.5cm)

CUTTING INSTRUCTIONS

Print cotton fabric scraps: Cut twenty-seven 5½in (14cm) squares

Cream cotton fabric: Cut two 3 x 42¾in (7.5 x 108.5cm) pieces, for the side borders

Cream cotton fabric: Cut two 3 x 20½in (7.5 x 52cm) pieces, for the top and bottom borders

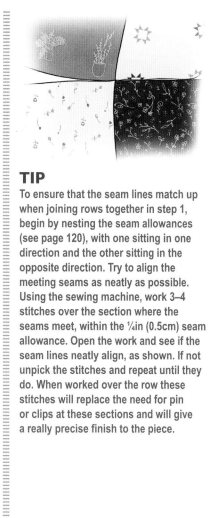

TIP

To ensure that the seam lines match up when joining rows together in step 1, begin by nesting the seam allowances (see page 120), with one sitting in one direction and the other sitting in the opposite direction. Try to align the meeting seams as neatly as possible. Using the sewing machine, work 3–4 stitches over the section where the seams meet, within the ¼in (0.5cm) seam allowance. Open the work and see if the seam lines neatly align, as shown. If not unpick the stitches and repeat until they do. When worked over the row these stitches will replace the need for pin or clips at these sections and will give a really precise finish to the piece.

1 Arrange nine 5½in (14cm) squares into three rows of three squares. Follow steps 1–5 on page 121 to sew the nine-square block. Press the entire block fully.

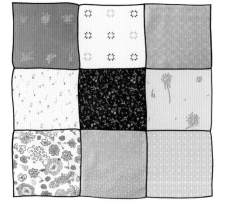

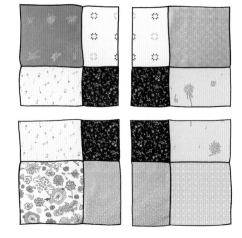

2 With a rotary cutter, ruler, and cutting mat, cut the block in half vertically. Then, without moving the pieces, cut it in half again horizontally. This will make four cut squares from the block.

3 Rearrange the four squares in the block until you are happy with the placement and the design created.

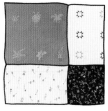

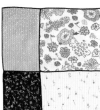
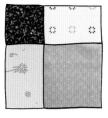

4 Place two squares in the top row together with their right sides facing and the raw edges aligned, and pin or clip in place. Sew together. Press the fabric open and the seam allowance to one side. Repeat to join the remaining two squares, pressing the seam allowance in the opposite direction.

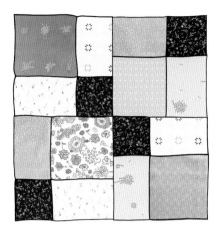

5 Place the two rows together with the right sides facing and the seams neatly nested. Pin or clip in place and sew together. Open to reveal the disappearing nine block and press fully. Repeat steps 1–5 to make two more blocks, so you have three disappearing nine blocks in total.

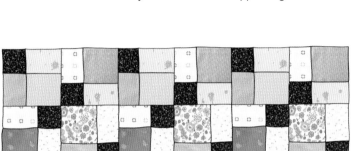

6 Arrange the blocks into a row. Sew the first two blocks together (see page 121), then repeat to join the remaining block. Press fully.

7 Place a long border strip along a long edge of the table runner with the right sides facing and the raw edges aligned. Pin or clip and then sew in place (see pages 18–19). Press open and press the seam allowance toward the border. Repeat with the second long border strip on the second long side.

8 Place a short border strip along a short edge of the table runner with the right sides facing and the raw edges aligned. Pin or clip and then sew in place. Press open and press the seam allowances towards the border. Repeat for the final short end of the runner. Press the panel fully.

9 Press the backing fabric and place it with its wrong side uppermost. Spray a small amount of adhesive on the batting and then position it on top, smoothing out any wrinkles, to baste the backing and batting together.

10 Apply a small amount of spray adhesive to the upper side of the batting. Layer the table runner on top with the right side uppermost, leaving a 4in (10cm) border of batting and backing fabrics around each side of the table runner top.

11 Sew quilting lines on the table runner as desired. Here the table runner has been machine quilted with a straight lines around the patchwork panel, and diagonal lines have been sewn across the square blocks.

12 Using a rotary cutter, ruler, and mat, carefully trim away the excess backing fabric and batting around the edge of the table runner and square up the sides as needed.

13 Follow the steps on page 123 to attach the binding around the outer edge of the quilt.

Finishing
Trim any excess threads and press lightly to neaten.

star pillow cover

The Sawtooth star is a traditional quilting block, and this version is made using Half Square Triangles worked in cool green tones. The simple envelope-style cover means that you can slip it on and off a pillow form with ease for laundering.

FABRIC AND MATERIALS
Cotton fabric scraps in a selection of four solid colors

Cotton backing fabric

Medium-loft fusible batting (wadding), Vlieseline H640, 18in (45.7cm) square

Coordinating thread

16in (40cm) square pillow form (cushion pad)

TOOLS AND EQUIPMENT
Basic quilting kit (see page 6)

FINISHED MEASUREMENTS
17in (43cm) square

CUTTING INSTRUCTIONS
Cotton fabric scraps:

Fabric A (cream): Cut four 4in (10cm) squares

Fabric A (cream): Cut four 5in (12.7cm) squares

Fabric B (dark blue): Cut four 5in (12.7cm) squares

Fabric C (light blue): Cut two 5in (12.7cm) squares

Fabric D (aqua): Cut two 5in (12.7cm) squares

Fabric A (cream): Cut two 1¾ x 16in (4.5 x 40.6cm) pieces and two 1¾ x 18in (4.5 x 45.7cm) pieces, for the border

Cotton backing fabric (cream, fabric A): Cut two 12 x 17in (30 x 43.2cm) pieces

1 Using the 5in (12.7cm) squares, follow steps 1–4 on page 122 to make eight Fabric A and Fabric B Half Square Triangles and four Fabric C and Fabric D HST. Press the seam allowances toward the darker fabrics.

2 Follow the photo opposite and the design in step 5 to lay out the HST and the 4in (10cm) squares into four rows of four squares to form the star motif. Follow step 2 on page 121 to join the first pair of squares together in the first row, followed by the second pair of squares. Repeat to join all of the pairs in turn.

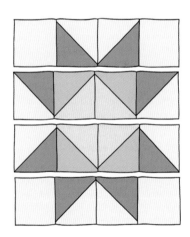

3 Join each of the pairs to make rows. Press the seam allowances in alternate directions (see page 121).

4 Working with pairs of rows at a time, join all the rows together, nesting the seams (see page 120). Carefully press the seams downward and press the whole panel.

5 Follow steps 6–7 on pages 18–19 to add the border strips, starting with the short strips for the top and bottom of the star panel, followed by the two long side border strips. Press fully and press all the seams toward the star panel.

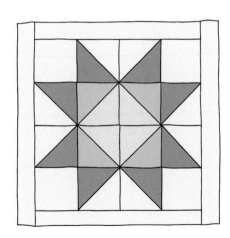

6 Place the completed star block with its right side uppermost onto the fusible batting and bond in place with an iron. Allow to cool.

7 Fold a short side of one of the backing panels to the wrong side by ½in (1.3cm) and press. Fold it to the wrong side by ½in (1.3cm) again and press. Sew in place with a straight machine stitch. Repeat for the second backing panel.

8 Place the star panel right side up and place the two backing panels on top with their right sides facing down, so their hemmed sides overlap in the center of the panel. Align the raw edges. Pin or clip in place. Sew around the four sides with a ½in (1.3cm) seam allowance before turning through.

Making up and finishing

Trim any excess threads and press lightly to neaten. Insert the pillow form into the cover.

TIPS

This design uses Half Square Triangles worked using a two-at-a-time method; however, you can work in your preferred method to create the HST for this project.

As this pillow cover features pale fabrics, be sure to press the seam allowances neatly toward the darker fabrics where possible to prevent them from showing on the right side of the finished piece.

placemat

This scrap-friendly project is a great way to use up left-over print cottons. Border the patchwork design with a solid cotton to frame the whimsical prints. As well as being used to quilt the project, the batting helps to protect your table when serving hot meals.

FABRIC AND MATERIALS

Cotton fabric scraps in a selection of prints

Cotton chambray, 18 x 10in (45.7 x 25.4cm), for the front

Cotton chambray, 18 x 13in (45.7 x 33cm), for the backing

Low-loft polyester batting (wadding), Vlieseline Thermolam, 11½ x 17½in (29.2 x 44.5cm)—use two pieces per mat for more heat protection

Coordinating thread

TOOLS AND EQUIPMENT

Basic sewing kit (see page 6)

Heat- or water-erasable marker

Spray adhesive (optional)

Poking tool or knitting needle

Hand-sewing needle

FINISHED MEASUREMENTS

11 x 16½in (28 x 42cm)

CUTTING INSTRUCTIONS

Print cotton fabric scraps: Cut five 4½ x 4in (11.5 x 10cm) pieces

Cotton chambray: Cut one 17½ x 3½in (44.5 x 9cm) piece, for the front Top Panel

Cotton chambray: Cut one 17½ x 4½in (44.5 x 11.5cm) piece, for the front Bottom Panel

Cotton chambray: Cut one 17½ x 11½in (44.5 x 29.2cm) piece, for the Backing

1 Arrange the print-cotton squares in your preferred order for the center strip. Place the first two squares together with their right sides facing, pin in place, then sew together (see page 121). Open the fabrics and press the seam allowance open. Continue to join the squares in the manner to until all the squares have been joined into a strip of five. Press fully.

2 Place the Top Panel onto the upper long edge of the strip with the right sides facing. Align the raw edges and pin or clip in place. Sew along the raw edge, press the fabrics open, and press the seam allowance toward the Top panel.

3 Place the Bottom Panel onto the lower long edge of the strip with the right sides facing. Align the raw edges and pin or clip in place. Sew along the raw edge, press the fabrics open, and press the seam allowance toward the Bottom panel.

TIP

These placemats use Vlieseline Thermolam—a thin polyester batting that has great heat-insulating properties—which helps to prevent heat from dishes marking the table beneath. Two layers of Thermolam are recommended to protect surfaces from heat. Be sure to test the batting with heat to ensure its suitability for your intended use.

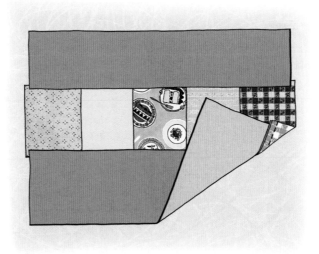

4 Spray one side of a piece of batting with adhesive, then add a second layer of batting on top if desired. Spray the top surface of the second layer lightly, then position the panel on top. Press to baste the layers together.

TIP
You can adapt this design to make smaller or larger placemats by simply increasing or decreasing the sizes of the fabric squares and borders. You could even scale these down to make a matching set of coasters.

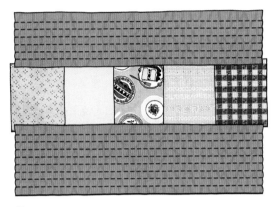

5 Using a walking foot on the sewing machine, sew straight quilting lines on the Top and Bottom Panels. You can work these freehand using the edge of the presser foot as a guide, or you can mark the lines with a heat- or water-erasable marker and use them as stitch guides.

6 With the placemat right side uppermost, position the backing piece on top, ensuring that the right sides of the fabrics are facing and the raw edges are aligned. Pin or clip on place.

7 Sew around the outer edge of the placemat, leaving a 2–3in (5–7.5cm) gap in the center of the long lower seam of the placemat. Use a pair of sharp scissors to trim away the excess seam allowance at the corners (see page 119).

8 Turn the placemat to the right side through the gap in the seam. Use a poking tool or a knitting needle to push out the corners fully. Press the seam allowance along the gap inward and press the whole placemat fully.

9 Hand-sew the gap in the seam allowance closed using ladder stitch (see page 124). Machine-sew around the outer edge of the placemat, taking a ¼in (0.5cm) seam allowance.

Finishing

Trim any excess threads and press lightly to neaten.

hanging wall organizer

Patchwork and quilting require a few specialist tools, so having them all to hand will enhance your sewing. This simple yet practical hanging wall tidy makes use of a large square embroidery hoop to stow your favorite quilting tools, so they are right where you need them!

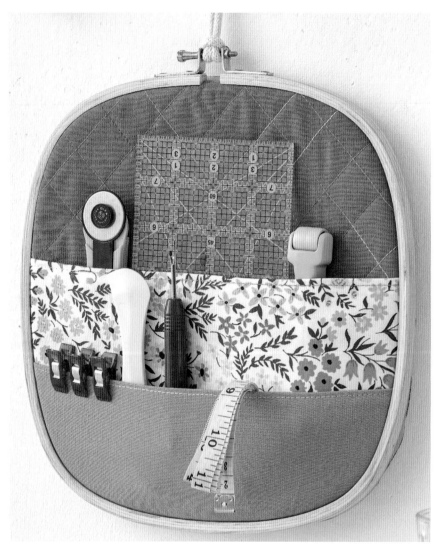

FABRIC AND MATERIALS

Cotton fabric scraps in a selection of solid colors and prints

Medium-loft fusible batting (wadding), Vlieseline H640, 14in (35.5cm) square

Fusible woven interlining, Vlieseline G700, 14in (35.5cm) square

Firm fusible interlining, Vlieseline Decovil 1 Light (or felt), 11in (28cm) square, for the backing

Cotton backing fabric (pink), 14in (35.5cm) square

Cotton cord, 12in (30cm)

Coordinating thread

Square embroidery hoop, 10in (25cm) wide

TOOLS AND EQUIPMENT

Basic sewing kit (see page 6)

Heat- or water-erasable marker

Hand-sewing needle

Craft glue (if using felt for the backing)

FINISHED MEASUREMENTS

10in (25cm) square

CUTTING INSTRUCTIONS

Print cotton: Cut one 7 x 14in (18 x 35.5cm) piece, for Pocket 1

Solid-color cotton (green): Cut one 5 x 14in (13 x 35.5cm) piece, for Pocket 2

Fusible woven interlining: Cut one 7in x 14in (18 x 35.5cm) piece and one 5 x 14in (13 x 35.5cm) piece

1 Place the background fabric wrong side down onto the fusible side of the batting and fuse into place, following the manufacturer's instructions. Set aside and allow to cool fully. Sew your desired quilt lines onto the fabric. Here the panel is quilted using variegated thread and worked in a straight-line geometric pattern using a walking foot.

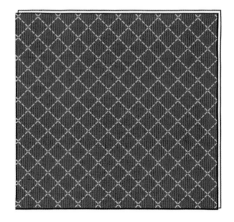

2 Press each pocket piece fully. Place the matching interlining piece onto the wrong side of each pocket piece. Cover with a pressing cloth, fuse into place with an iron, and allow to cool fully.

3 Fold a long edge of one of the pocket pieces to the wrong side by ¼in (0.5cm) and press. Secure with pins or clips. Sew along the upper edge of the folded section to secure in place. Repeat for the second pocket piece.

4 Prepare the backing by placing the outer part of the embroidery hoop onto the Decovil 1 Light Interlining or thick felt. With a water- or heat-erasable marker, carefully draw around the outer edge of the embroidery frame and cut the piece out. Set aside.

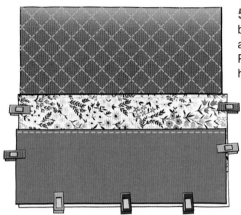

5 Layer the pockets onto the quilted backing panel, aligning the raw edges and ensuring the pockets are level. Pin or clip around the outer edge to hold the layers securely in place.

TIP
You can customize this design by adding another pocket or working a line of stitching vertically through the pockets to make a divider for each item.

TIP
Before securing the layers of fabric in the embroidery frame, ensure that the screw fastening is unscrewed as much as possible. This will allow the top section to be opened wide enough to fit the layers. Once the back of the embroidery frame is in position, tighten the screw fastening.

6 Separate the two parts of the embroidery frame. Position the quilted panel onto the inner part of the frame. Aim to get the pockets as level as possible. With the outer part of the frame opened as wide as possible, place it on top and gently press into place. Once you're happy with the placement, fasten the screw to secure the frame in place.

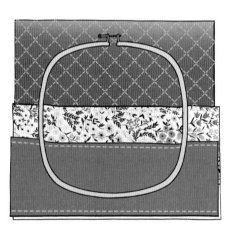

7 Use large scissors to trim away the excess panel to leave a 2in (5cm) border around the frame. You can trim down the batting even more to reduce the bulk as needed. With a needle and thread, work two lines of long gather stitches (see page 124) around the border fabric, then draw up to pull the fabric in toward the center of the back of the work. Fasten off securely.

8 Place the backing panel onto the back of the work. If using Decovil 1 Light, carefully fuse it into place or if using felt, apply glue to secure it around the edges.

9 Create a hanging loop by folding the 12in (30cm) length of cotton cord in half and pushing it through the screw fixing at the top of the embroidery frame. Pass the ends through to create a lark's head knot. Knot the ends together to finish.

Finishing
Trim any excess threads and press lightly to neaten.

festive quilt

This quilt is made using an Economy Block which is surprisingly quick and fun to make. The block is great for using up scraps and you can follow the tip on page 17 to fussy cut your fabrics to showcase a cacophony of festive prints.

FABRIC AND MATERIALS

Cotton fabrics in a selection of approx. 10 festive prints for A and B, each 9 x 22in (23 x 56cm)—this is known as a Fat Eighth (see page 5)

Cotton fabrics in a selection of low-volume prints for C, approx. 40 x 30in (102 x 76cm)

Cotton backing fabric, 45in (114cm) square

Binding, 170in (430cm)

Batting (wadding), 45in (114cm) square

Coordinating thread

TOOLS AND EQUIPMENT

Basic sewing kit (see page 6)

Rotating cutting mat (optional, see tip)

Quilting safety pins (curved)

Quilt basting thread and needle

FINISHED MEASUREMENTS

40in (101.5cm) square

CUTTING INSTRUCTIONS

Print cotton fabrics: Cut twenty-five 4½in (11.5cm) squares for the center of the blocks (A)

Print cotton fabrics: Cut twenty-five 5½in (14cm) squares. Cut each one in half diagonally, then in half diagonally again to make four small triangles (B)

Low-volume cotton fabrics: Cut fifty 5in (12.7cm) squares. Cut each one in half diagonally to make two triangles (C). Four of these will be needed per block.

1 Lay out the elements for one block. Each block will require a center square (A) four small triangles (B) and four large triangles (C)

  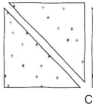

A   B   C

2 In the first round of the block, the small triangles are secured to the sides of the center square. Begin by folding the square in half and then half again, and finger-press the folds. Fold the small triangles in half and finger-press to form a crease. These crease lines will allow you to neatly position the elements to be joined.

3 Position a small triangle (B) onto a center square (A) with the right sides facing. Align the crease lines and pin in place. Sew together and finger-press the fabric open. Press the seam allowance toward the triangle.

4 Place the second triangle on the opposite side of the square in the same manner, aligning the raw edges and the creases. Pin in place. Sew together, then finger-press the fabric open. Press the seam allowance toward the triangle.

5 Place the third triangle on the bottom of the center square in the same manner. Sew together, finger-press the fabric open, and press the seam allowance toward the triangle. Join the final triangle to the top of the center square and press in the same manner.

TIPS

The block featured in this quilt—the Economy Block—is surprising easy to make and once you've worked a few you'll find the quilt top comes together really quickly! You can work in a repeated pattern of colors or use a wide range of fabrics for a truly scrappy style.

A small rotating cutting mat is a useful addition to your quilting supplies. For this project it makes it easier to cut the four small triangles more accurately from a square without moving the fabrics too much. Simply cut along one diagonal, rotate the mat, and make the second cut.

This design creates Economy Blocks that are 8in (20cm) square, but you can increase the size of the quilt by working more blocks, and increase the number of blocks in a row and rows in the finished quilt. You could also sew four blocks together to make a matching pillow cover.

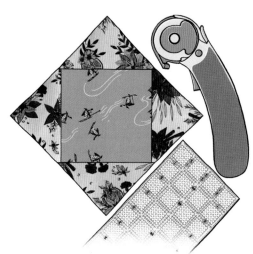

6 Press the whole block fully. Using a rotary cutter, ruler, and cutting mat square up the block and remove the excess points at the seam allowances.

7 Working with four larger triangles (C), fold each one in half and finger-press to form crease lines. Place the first large triangle onto the block with the right sides facing. Align the raw edges and the center crease lines and pin in place. Sew together, finger-press the fabric open, and press the seam allowance toward the triangle.

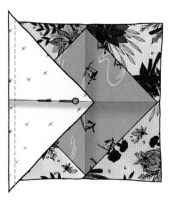

8 Place the second large triangle onto the block on the opposite side with the right sides facing, and follow step 7 to join and press in the same manner. Repeat to join the third and fourth large triangles to the top and bottom edges of the block. Press the pieces open, and press the seam allowances toward the triangle.

9 Press the block fully and using a rotary cutter, ruler, and cutting mat, trim away the excess seam allowance and square up as needed. Repeat steps 2–9 to make a further 24 blocks, so you have 25 blocks in total.

10 Place the blocks into five rows of five blocks and arrange until you are happy with the placement. Follow steps 2–4 on page 121 to join the squares of each row and press the seam allowances in alternate directions.

11 Follow steps 5–6 on page 121 to join the rows together to complete the quilt top. Press all the seam allowances downward.

12 Place the backing fabric with wrong side uppermost and position the batting on top. Place the quilt top on top with its right side uppermost, leaving a border of batting around the quilt top.

13 Baste (tack) in place as preferred with curved safety pin or long basting stitches (see tip on page 124). Quilt as desired. Here this quilt has been worked with straight lines to emphasize the design.

14 Using a rotary cutter and ruler carefully trim away the excess backing fabric and batting around the quilt and square up as needed.

15 Follow the steps on page 123 to attach the binding around the outer edge of the quilt.

Finishing
Trim any excess threads and press lightly to neaten.

single block wall hanging

Quilts are usually made up of a pattern of blocks repeated over and over, but in isolation the blocks themselves are often striking and work as stand-alone designs. This mini quilt is made from a single Churn Dash block worked in statement colors.

FABRIC AND MATERIALS

Cotton fabric scraps in a selection of prints for the center square, motif, and background

Cotton backing fabric, 20in (51cm) square

Scraps of cotton fabric for the hanging tabs

Medium-weight non-woven fusible interlining, Vlieseline H250, 4in (10cm) square

Binding, 70in (178cm)

Batting (wadding), 20in (51cm) square

Coordinating thread

TOOLS AND EQUIPMENT

Basic sewing kit (see page 6)

Spray adhesive (optional)

Wooden doweling, 14½in (37cm), for hanging your quilt

FINISHED MEASUREMENTS

15¼in (39cm) square

TIPS

This mini quilt is made with a single block, the Churn Dash, but you can swap it out for a different block if you prefer. You could create a series of single block mini quilts and display them on your wall as a collection.

Working with contrasting fabric makes a single motif really shine. You can opt for modern fabric designs or even bright clashing tones. The center square, as show here, is a great place to showcase or fussy cut (see page 17) a bold print.

Print cotton fabric scraps:

Fabric A: Cut one 4½in (11.5cm) square for the center square

Fabric B (contrast fabric): Cut two 5in (12.7cm) squares and four 2½ x 4½in (6.5 x 11.5cm) pieces

Fabric C (background fabric): Cut two 5in (12.7cm) squares and four 2½ x 4½in (6.5 x 11.5cm) pieces

Fabric C (background fabric): Cut two 15¼ x 1¾in (38.7 x 4.5cm) pieces for the side borders

Fabric C (background fabric): Cut two 12 x 1¾in (30 x 4.5cm) pieces for the top and bottom

Cotton fabric scraps: Cut two 4in (10cm) squares for the hanging tabs

Medium-weight non-woven fusible interlining: Cut the square in half diagonally to make two triangles

1 Lay out the cut fabrics and set out the pieces that will form the motif (Fabric B) and the background (Fabric C). Place a Fabric B and Fabric C square together with the right sides facing and follow steps 1–4 on page 122 to make two Half Square Triangles. Repeat with the remaining Fabric B and C squares to make two more HST.

2 Place a Fabric B and C rectangle together with the right sides facing and pin in place. Sew along one long edge. Open the fabric to reveal a square of the two fabrics. Press the seam allowance toward the darker fabric. Repeat to make three more of these squares, so you have four in total.

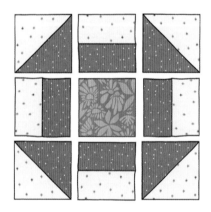

3 Arrange the nine squares into three rows of three. The background and the contrast fabric form the motif that is positioned around the center square.

4 Follow steps 2–7 on page 121 to sew the nine-block square together. Press the block fully, pressing the seam allowances downwards.

5 Place one of the short border strips along the upper edge of the block with the right sides facing. Pin or clip then sew in place. Press fully, pressing the seam allowance toward the border. Repeat to sew the second short border strip to the lower edge of the block.

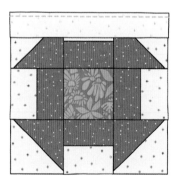

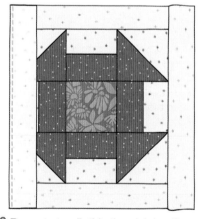

6 Repeat step 5, this time joining the long border pieces to each side of the block in turn.

7 Press the backing fabric fully and place it with its wrong side uppermost. Spray a small amount of adhesive onto one side of the batting, then position it on the backing fabric. Spray the other side of the batting lightly. Place the block right side up on top, leaving an even border of batting around the edge. Press to baste the layers together.

8 Quilt as desired. Here the project has been quilted using straight lines worked with a walking foot to echo the motif. Use a rotary cutter and ruler to trim away the excess batting and backing fabrics and square up as needed.

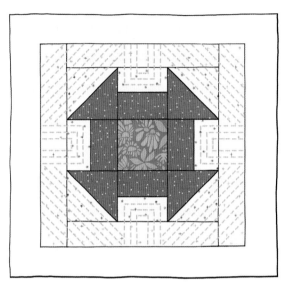

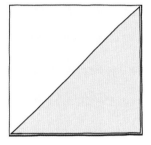

9 Place the a cotton square for one of the hanging tabs with its wrong side uppermost. Position the interlining triangle on top, aligning the raw edges. The interlining will only cover half of the square. Cover with a pressing cloth and fuse into place. Leave to cool fully.

10 Fold the cotton over to conceal the interlining and press fully. Repeat steps 9 and 10 to make the second triangle.

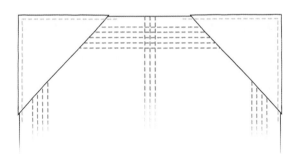

11 Place a triangle into each of the upper corners on the back of the block, aligning the raw edges of the triangle with the raw edges of the quilt top. Pin or clip in place. Sew in place along the corners of the quilt top, within the ¼in (0.5cm) seam allowance. Press the quilt fully.

12 Follow the steps on page 123 to attach the binding around the outer edge of the quilt.

Finishing
Trim any excess threads and press lightly to neaten. On the back of the work, slide the doweling under the two upper corner tabs for hanging.

color block wall hanging

This mini quilted wall hanging plays with layers and textures to create a contemporary quilted textile art piece. The simple design is made by layering quilted pieces together and shaping them for a softer finish.

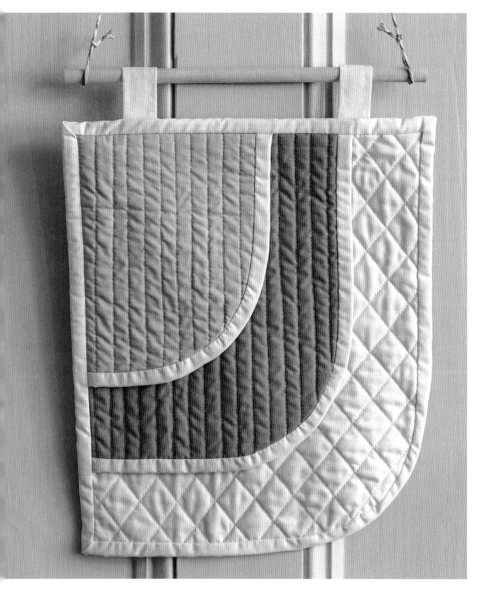

FABRIC AND MATERIALS

Cotton fabrics in a selection of solid colors:
    Blue: approx. 15 x 20 (38 x 51cm)
    Peach: approx. 20 x 24in (51 x 61cm)
    Cream: approx. 25 x 30in (63.5 x 76cm)

Cream cotton fabric, 2½ x 16in (6.5 x 40.5cm), for the hanging tabs

Medium-weight non-woven fusible interlining, 1 x 16in (2.5 x 40.5cm)

Binding, 130in (330cm)

Batting (wadding), 35in (90cm) square

Coordinating thread

TOOLS AND EQUIPMENT

Basic sewing kit (see page 6)

Walking foot

Spray adhesive (optional)

Large bowl or plate

Wooden doweling, 14in (35.5cm)

Glue stick

FINISHED MEASUREMENTS

12 x 14in (30 x 35.5cm)

CUTTING INSTRUCTIONS

Blue fabric: Cut two 7 x 9in (17.8 x 22.8cm) pieces

Peach fabric: Cut two 12 x 10in (30 x 25.5cm) pieces

Cream fabric: Cut two 12 x 14in (30 x 35.5cm) pieces

Fabric for tabs: Cut two 2½ x 8in (6.5 x 20cm) pieces

Interlining: Cut two 1 x 8in (2.5 x 20cm) pieces

Batting: Cut one 7 x 9in (17.8 x 22.8cm) piece, one 12 x 10in (30 x 25.5cm) piece, and one 12 x 14in (30 x 35.5cm) piece

1 Create the larger panel by placing a cream cotton piece with its right side facing down. Place the matching batting piece on top, then place the second cream cotton piece on top with its right side facing up. Use spray adhesive to baste (tack) the cotton fabrics to the batting as needed (see tip on page 55). Quilt the design as desired. This panel has been quilted using a straight-line geometric diamond design worked with a walking foot.

2 Follow step 1 to make the blue and peach panels in the same manner.

3 Use a large bowl or plate to mark a curve on the lower right-hand corner of the cream panel. Cut along the curve with sharp scissors. Repeat for the blue and peach panels.

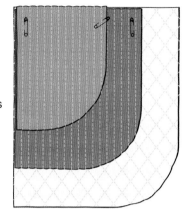

4 Layer the cream and peach quilted panels together, aligning the straight edges, and pin or clip in place. Place the blue panel on top of the work, aligning the straight edges and pin or clip in place. Curved quilting pins will be better than pins or clips for holding together the thick layers of this project. Check the placement and trim the pieces down as needed.

5 Unpin the pieces. Working on the smallest panel first, position the binding around the curved side of the panel. Pin, clip or use the glue stick to glue baste in place. The straight edges will be bound in the final step.

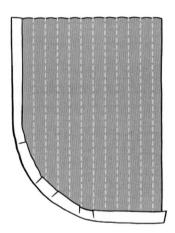

6 Machine-sew the binding to the right side of the quilt piece, working the stitches into the fold of the binding (see page 123). Fold the binding over to the back of the panel and hand-sew in place using ladder stitch (see page 124).

7 Repeat steps 5 and 6 for the medium-sized quilted panel.

8 Layer the three panels together in the same way as step 4 and pin or clip in place.

9 Position the binding around the whole of the outer panel—this will include all three panels on the straight edges. Follow the steps on page 123 to attach the binding around the outer edge of the quilt.

10 Fuse one piece of the interlining to the wrong side of a hanging-tab strip and allow to cool fully. Fold each of the long sides to the wrong side of the fabric by ¼in (0.5cm) and press. Fold the strip in half so the long sides meet and press again, so the raw edges are concealed. Fold the tab in half so the two short edges meet, to make a loop. Fold the raw edge over to one side by ⅜in (1cm). Repeat to make the second hanging tab.

TIPS

This design features three layers of quilted pieces stacked together. Using the walking foot attachment and increasing the stitch length to 3.5–4 will make it easier when sewing through these bulky layers.

Each of these panels have the same backing fabric as the front of the work. This means that you can work with a single piece of fabric folded over or two pieces layered to make each part of the design.

11 Evenly space the hanging tabs on the back of the quilt, so their raw edges are facing the back of the quilt. Hand-stitch the tabs to the back of the quilt.

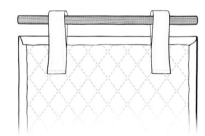

Making up and finishing

Trim any excess threads and press lightly to neaten. Slide the doweling into the two hanging tabs.

reading book pillow

Bookworms will tell you there is nothing better than curling up with a good book. This pillow is the ideal addition to a child's room or a cozy reading nook, and you can stow a book or pair of pajamas in the pocket safely till next time, too!

FABRIC AND MATERIALS

Cotton fabric scraps in a selection of solid colors (I used pink, blue, orange, green, and cream)

Cream cotton fabric

Print cotton

Medium-loft fusible batting (wadding), Vlieseline H640, 18 x 12in (45.7 x 30cm)

Coordinating thread

Pillow form (cushion pad), 16in (40cm) square

TOOLS AND EQUIPMENT

Basic quilting kit (see page 6)

Rotating cutting mat (optional)

FINISHED MEASUREMENTS

17in (43cm) square

CUTTING INSTRUCTIONS

Cotton fabric scraps in solid colors:

Cut two 3½in (9cm) squares in each of the pink, blue, orange, green, and cream fabrics, for the Half Square Triangles

Cream cotton fabric:

Cut six 4½ x 1in (11.5 x 2.5cm) strips and one 18 x 2½in (45.5 x 6.5cm) strip, for the sashing

Cut two 11in x 2½in (28 x 6.5cm) strips and one 18 x 2½in (45.5 x 6.5cm) strip, for the border

Cut one 18 x 14in (45.5 x 35.5cm) piece, for the pocket backing

Print cotton:

Cut one 17in (43cm) square, for the front

Cut two 12 x 17in (30 x 43cm) pieces, for the back

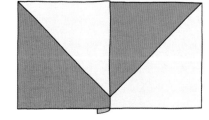

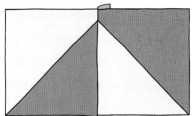

1 Select a colored square and a cream square for the pinwheel blocks. Follow steps 1–3 on page 122 to make four Half Square Triangles (HST) using the four-block method (see tip on page 95).

2 Arrange the four HST in two rows of two blocks to create a pinwheel design. Seam the pair of squares in each row together (see page 121). Press the seam allowances in opposite directions (see page 121).

3 Place the two pairs together with the right sides facing and pin or clip in place. Sew together then press the block fully. Use a rotary cutter and ruler to square up to neaten.

4 Repeat steps 1–3 to make seven more pinwheel blocks, so you have eight in total. Arrange the blocks into two rows of four squares.

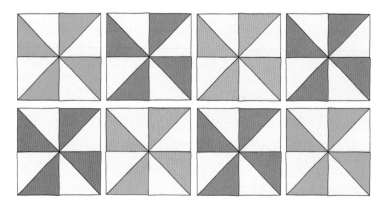

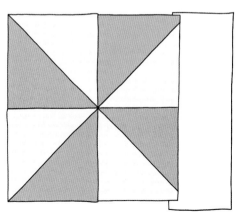

5 Place a small sashing piece onto the first block in one of the rows with the right sides facing, aligning the raw edges. Pin or clip in place. Sew in place and press neatly open.

TIPS

While this design has been made in fun child-friendly prints, there is no reason you can't make a more grown-up version by switching out the prints.

When using the four-at-a-time Half Square Triangle method, a rotating cutting mat is great tool. You can carefully rotate the work and make the second cut without shifting the pieces that have already been cut, allowing you to cut with both ease and precision.

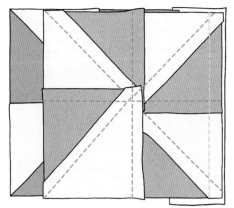

6 Place the next pinwheel block in the row on top of the sashing with the right sides facing. Align the raw edges and pin or clip in place. Sew in place, then press the block open.

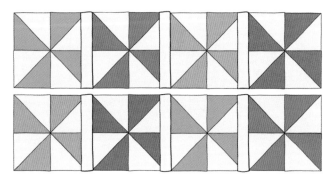

7 Continue in this manner, joining sashing strips between the blocks to create two rows of four blocks. Press them fully.

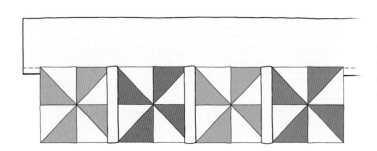

8 Place the wider sashing piece onto the long edge of the bottom row of pinwheels with the right sides facing and the raw edges aligned. Pin or clip in place. Sew in place and press open.

9 Repeat to secure the top pinwheel panel onto the other side of the wide sashing and press open.

10 Place a short border piece onto a short end of the panel with the right sides facing and the raw edges aligned and pin in place. Sew together and press open. Repeat for the second short side.

11 Follow step 10 to join the long border panel to the lower side of the pinwheel panel. Press open and press the panel fully.

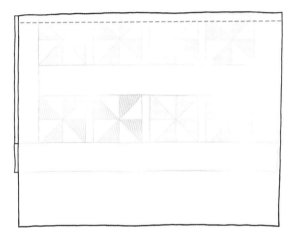

12 Position the pocket backing in place along the upper edge of the pinwheel panel with the right sides facing and pin or clip in place. Sew in place and press open. This section will be larger than the pinwheel panel as it forms the top border of the panel and covers the inside of the pocket. Turn the piece over so it is wrong side uppermost.

13 Place the fusible batting onto the wrong side of the pinwheel panel. Align it with the bottom edge of the lower border of the pinwheel panel and fuse in place. The batting will only cover part of the pocket backing. Press fully. Fold the pocket backing over the batting so it meets the lower edge of the pocket. Position the finished pocket onto the print-cotton square for the pillow front. Pin or clip in place and set aside.

14 Take a backing panel and fold one of its long edges to the wrong side of the fabric by ½in (1.3cm) and press. Fold this edge to the wrong side by ½in (1.3cm) again and press. Sew the folded edge in place. Repeat for the second backing panel.

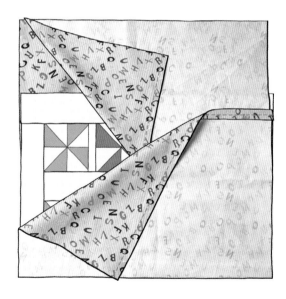

15 Place the two backing panels onto the front piece and pocket section, so the right sides are facing. Align the raw edges—the backing panels will overlap at the center. Pin or clip in place.

16 Sew around all four sides of the pillow cover, using a ½in (1.3cm) seam allowance, before turning through to the right side.

Making up and finishing
Trim any excess threads and press lightly to neaten. Insert the pillow form into the cover.

lightning bolt wall hanging

This high-impact quilt inspired by Ziggy Stardust is a foundation paper piece project. The design is mapped out onto paper, which is used as a placement and stitching guide for the fabrics before it is ultimately ripped out.

FABRIC AND MATERIALS

Cotton fabric scraps in a selection of solid colors—I used pink and turquoise

Low volume cotton fabric, 22 x 30in (56 x 76cm), for the background and backing

Medium-loft fusible batting (wadding), Vlieseline H640, 8¼ x 11½in (21 x 29.2cm)

Poster/print hanging frame, 8in (20cm)

Coordinating thread

Light box (optional, see tip below)

TOOLS AND EQUIPMENT

Basic sewing kit (see page 6)

Glue stick (optional)

Light box (optional)

Seam roller (optional)

TEMPLATES (SEE PAGE 127)

Lightning bolt units A, B, and C

FINISHED MEASUREMENTS

8¼ x 11½in (21 x 29cm)

NOTE

When using the templates, the fabrics are placed on the back (the unmarked side) and the stitching is worked on the printed side. Here the template and fabric scraps are shown on a light box, so they appear translucent in the step illustrations.

1 Place the paper template for unit A right-side down on the light box. Place the first scrap of fabric onto the template on space 1. Ensure that the fabric covers all of space 1. Use a small dab of glue to hold the fabric in pace as needed.

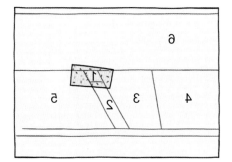

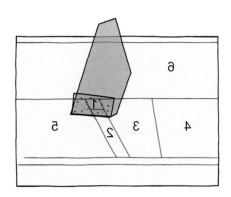

2 Position the second fabric scrap following the numbered guide on the chart. Check that the second fabric scrap will cover space 2. Position the fabric so the right sides of the two pieces are facing, and so that when you stitch the line at the bottom of space 1, the second scrap will fold down to cover space 2.

TIP

When working a foundation paper piece project, the fabrics are positioned on the opposite side to the printed template. Using a light box can help you with the precise placement of the fabric. If you don't have access to a light box, holding the elements up to a light source will help to assess if the placement of the fabric is correct.

3 Pin the second scrap in place, ensuring the pin is away from the horizontal line at the bottom of space 1. Turn the work over so that the template is uppermost. Sew along the horizontal line at the bottom of space 1 on the template to join the fabrics (see tip on page 115).

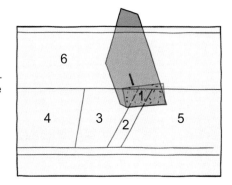

4 Fold the template along the stitch line and finger press or press the fold with a seam roller. Using a rotary cutter and ruler, cut away the excess fabric to create a ¼in (0.5cm) seam allowance from the folded edge of the template.

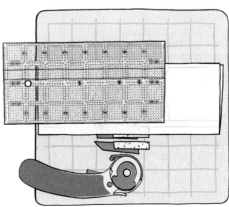

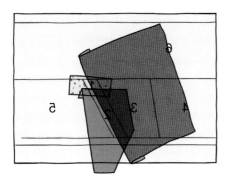

5 Place the template with the fabric side uppermost. Position the next piece of fabric, wrong side down, over space 3. Check that the fabric will cover space 3 and then fold one of its raw edges so this edge will extend beyond the right-hand side of space 2.

6 Fold the third piece of fabric down so its right side is facing the first two pieces. Pin or glue in place. Turn the work over again so the template is uppermost. Sew along the left-hand side of space 2 to secure the fabrics.

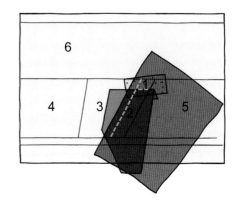

7 Fold back the template along the stitch line and finger press or press it with a seam roller. As you did in step 4, trim away the excess fabric to give a ¼in (0.5cm) seam allowance from the folded edge of the template.

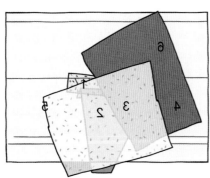

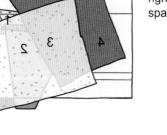

8 Turn the template over again so the fabrics are uppermost. Position the next piece of fabric right-side down on the work, so that it will cover space 4 when folded over. Pin in place.

9 Turn the work over so the template is uppermost. Sew the fourth piece of fabric place along the line on the right-hand side of space 4.

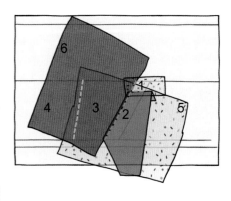

10 Fold back the template along the stitch line and finger press or press it with a seam roller. As you did in step 4, trim away the excess fabric to give a ¼in (0.5cm) seam allowance from the folded edge of the template.

11 Continue in the same manner to sew two more fabric scraps to cover spaces 5 and 6, and trim the seam allowances.

12 This completes unit A of the template. Make the other two units of the pattern in the same manner.

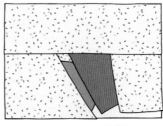

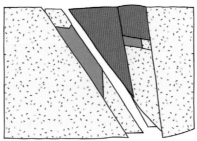

13 Press the three units fully and arrange in the correct placement ready to be joined.

14 Place units B and C together with the right sides facing, aligning the marked seam allowances, and pin in place. Sew the two units together.

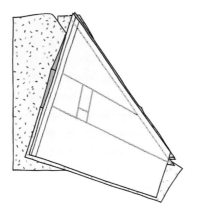

TIP
When using the paper piecing technique, reduce the stitch length to between 1.2 and 1.5—this will perforate the paper and will help you to remove it when the panel is completed.

15 Press the units open. The creates the lower part of the template. Trim away any excess fabric along the edges of the two sections and press the pieces fully.

16 Place unit A on top of the joined units B and C with the right sides facing. Align the marked seam allowance at the bottom of unit A with the seam allowance at the top of units B and C. Pin in place. Sew the two sections together.

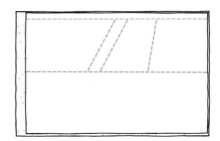

17 Remove the paper templates by carefully peeling them away and ripping them from the stitching. The paper should pull away easily—avoid tugging too hard as this can damage the stitching. If there is some resistance when pulling, simply use a clean paint brush and work over the stitching lines with water to help remove the papers.

18 Position the fusible batting centrally on the wrong side of the design, with the fusible side of the batting facing the wrong side of the panel. Cover with a pressing cloth and fuse into place. Allow to cool fully.

19 Place the work onto the backing fabric so the right sides are facing, and pin in place. Sew around all four sides, using the edge of the batting as a stitch guide and leaving a 2–3in (5–7.5cm) gap along the lower seam. Using a rotary cutter ruler and mat, trim away any excess fabric so you have a ¼in (0.5cm) seam allowance around the stitch line.

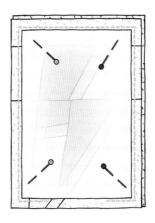

20 Using sharp scissors, clip away the bulk from the seam allowance at the corners (see page 119).

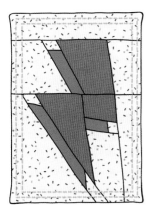

21 Turn the piece through to the right side through the gap in the seam allowance and push out the corners fully. Press the seam allowance inward at the gap and hand-sew the gap closed with ladder stitch (see page 124). Work two lines of topstitching (see page 119) around the outer edge of the design, the first line of stitching ¼in (0.5cm) from the edge and then the second line of stitching ½in (1.3cm) from the edge.

Making up and finishing
Trim any excess threads and press lightly to neaten.

Following the manufacturer's instructions, secure the poster frame to the top and bottom of the panel to finish.

stained glass quilt

Taking inspiration from stained glass windows, this style of quilting features small pieces of colored fabric with a thin border. Working in an improv-piecing style this is a great project for using up fabric offcuts and creating a truly unique piece.

FABRIC AND MATERIALS

Cotton fabric scraps in a selection of solid colors, including white for the sashing and border

Tear-away embroidery stabilizer, Vlieseline Stitch'n'Tear, 8 x 12in (20 x 30cm)

Medium-weight non-woven fusible interlining, Vlieseline H250, 4in (10cm) square

Cotton backing fabric, 24 x 20in (61 x 51cm)

Binding, 64in (162.5cm)

Batting (wadding), 15 x 20in (38 x 51cm)

Wooden doweling, 10in (25.5cm)

Coordinating thread

TOOLS AND EQUIPMENT

Basic sewing kit (see page 6)

Seam roller

Spray adhesive (optional)

Glue stick (optional)

FINISHED MEASUREMENTS

11¾ x 15in (30 x 38cm)

CUTTING INSTRUCTIONS

White cotton fabric scraps:

Cut one ¾ x 20in (2 x 51cm) strip, then cut it into four lengths of 5in (12.7cm), for the sashing

Cut one 1¼ x 20in (3.2 x 51cm) strip for center sashing

Cut two 1¾ x 12in (4.5 x 30cm) strips for side borders

Cut two 1¾ x 12in (4.5 x 30cm) strips for top and bottom borders

Cotton backing fabric:

Cut one 15 x 20in (38 x 51cm) piece for the backing

Cut two 4in (10cm) squares for the hanging tabs

Vlieseline Stitch'N' Tear: Cut six 4in (10cm) squares

Fusible interlining square: Cut diagonally to make two triangles

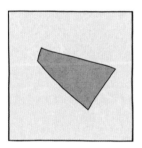

1 Place the first scrap of fabric onto the center of a Stitch 'n' Tear square. Secure it in place using the glue stick if desired.

2 With the right sides facing, place another fabric scrap on top, aligning the raw edges. Here the second piece is a long strip—the excess can be trimmed away as needed. Pin in place. Sew the two pieces together along the top long edge of the second piece.

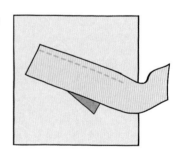

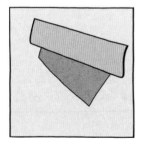

3 Open out the top piece and finger-press it flat or use a seam roller to press it. Trim away any excess fabric as needed.

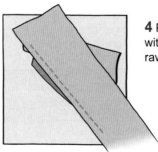

4 Place the next piece of fabric onto the work with the right sides facing, aligning the lower raw edges. Pin and then sew in place.

5 Finger press the fabric open, or use a seam roller, and trim away any excess fabric as needed.

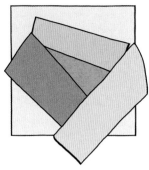

6 Place the next scrap of fabric onto the work with the right sides facing and pin and stitch in the same manner. Finger press fabric open, or use a seam roller.

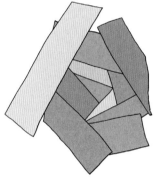

7 Continue adding fabric scraps in the same manner until the guide square has been covered. Here the fabrics have been worked around a center piece of fabric, but you can position the scraps in any orientation to cover the whole guide square.

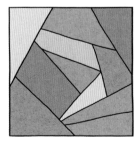

8 With a rotary cutter and ruler, trim away the excess fabric around the work and square up to make a neat 4in (10cm) square.

9 Repeat steps 1–8 to make five more blocks, so you have six in total. These blocks are all made by joining the pieces in turn but as the fabrics are all different sizes, the finished design of each of the blocks will be unique.

10 Carefully remove the stabilizer from the back of the blocks. While the stabilizer is designed to be torn away from the finished piece, be careful not to tug at the stitches as this can damage them.

TIP

The color palette you chose for your quilt can dramatically change the overall finish. Here muted pastels have been selected, but you could use neon bright colors for a bolder finish. Traditionally these designs are worked with black or dark bordering fabrics to resemble stained glass. Here the borders have been kept light and bright to ring the changes for this design.

11 Place the first 5in (12.7cm) sashing strip onto one side of a block with the right sides facing and pin or clip in place. Sew in place and press open fully.

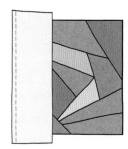

12 Place the next block on top with the right sides facing and align its raw edge with the raw edge of the sashing. Pin or clip in place. Sew in place and press open fully.

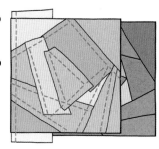

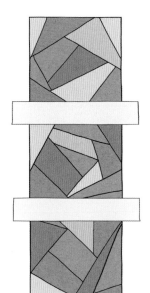

13 Repeat step 12 to join a third block to the row with sashing to complete the row. Press open fully.

14 Repeat steps 11–13 to join the three remaining blocks with the sashing to make a second row. Use a rotary cutter and ruler to trim away any excess sashing fabrics.

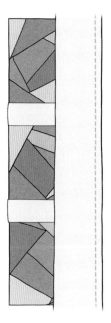

15 Place the long sashing strip onto one row with the right sides facing and the raw edges aligned. Pin or clip and then sew in place. Press fully open.

16 Position the second row onto the work with the right side facing. Align the raw edge with the raw edge of the sashing. Pin or clip and then sew in place. Press fully open.

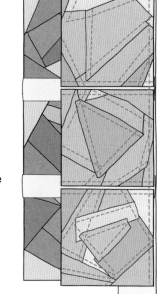

TIP

A tear-away embroidery stabilizer is used in this project as a guide for creating the blocks. This helps to create blocks that are the correct size and helps with the design and placement for the fabrics. You could instead use a very fine interlining or cotton and leave it in the work when it is finished.

17 Follow steps 5–6 on page 104 to sew border strips to each side of the panel, and then to the top and bottom of the panel. Press open fully.

18 Press the backing fabric with its wrong side uppermost. Spray a small amount of adhesive on the batting and press onto the backing fabric to baste it in place. Spray a small amount of adhesive onto the batting and press the quilt top into place.

19 Quilt as desired—here straight lines have been sewn, following the outlines of the patchwork panel.

20 Follow steps 9–11 on page 105 to make the triangular hanging tabs and sew them onto the top of the back of the quilt.

21 Follow the steps on page 123 to attach the binding around the outer edge of the quilt.

Making up and finishing

Trim any excess threads and press lightly to neaten.

On the back of the work, slide the doweling under the two upper corner tabs for hanging.

techniques

Here you'll find all the basic sewing and quilting techniques you'll need to make the projects in this book.

Basic sewing techniques

Topstitching

Topstitching is worked on the right side of the fabric and can be functional as well as decorative—holding pieces or a pocket in place, for example. It is a simple straight stitch set at a longer length than normal for greater impact. Depending on the effect you want to create, you could opt for a thread color that matches or contrasts with the fabric.

Stitch in the ditch

Using a straight stitch and working on the right side of the piece, stitch as close to the seam as you can get. When you have finished, the stitches should be barely visible, hidden by the ridge of the seam.

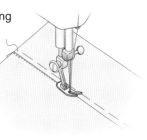

Pressing seams open

Using an iron, press over the seam in the direction in which it was stitched to embed the stitches. Press the seam open so the seam allowances lie flat, using your fingers to open out the seam edges as you press.

Reducing bulk

Clipping curved seams

Using a sharp pair of small pointed scissors, cut small wedges of fabric from the seam allowance around the curve at regular intervals, taking care to cut close to, but not through, the stitches.

Trimming an outward corner

Using a sharp pair of small pointed scissors, trim away the corner of fabric as shown, cutting close to the stitching but taking care not to cut through the stitches.

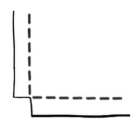

Snipping an inward corner

Using a sharp pair of small pointed scissors, snip as far into the angle as you can, taking care not to cut through the stitches.

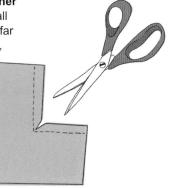

Applying fusible interlining (interfacing)

Lay the interlining piece, adhesive side down, on the wrong side of the fabric piece. Lay a pressing cloth over the top of the interlining and fabric, and press down firmly without using a gliding action. Remove the cloth and leave to cool fully, to ensure the pieces have bonded securely.

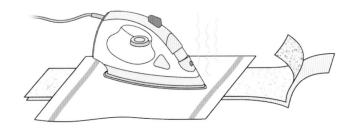

Quilting techniques

Cutting accurate fabric pieces

Squaring up

Whether you're using scraps or fabric bought from a shop, it will most likely not be 100 percent square. Starting with a squared-off corner will ensure your cuts are as precise as possible.

1 Press your fabric—this will ensure more accurate cutting.

2 Place the fabric right side up on a cutting mat, with a selvage edge at the top of the mat. If you're using scrap fabric and it doesn't have a selvage, cut along one side in the same direction as the fabric's threads to create a straight edge, and place the straight edge at the top of the mat. Place the quilter's ruler on the fabric so a little of the fabric sticks out to the right of the ruler. Align one of the horizontal marks on the ruler with the selvage or straight edge.

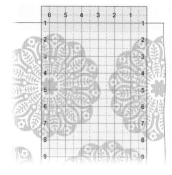

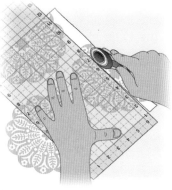

3 With your left hand, press down firmly on the ruler. With your right hand, press firmly on the rotary cutter and, starting nearest your body, push the cutter away from you through the fabric. You will end up with a perfect 90-degree corner.

Cutting fabric squares

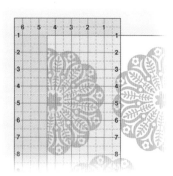

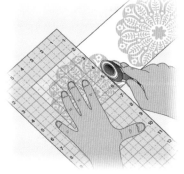

1 Here we are cutting 4½in (11.5cm) strips from a fat quarter. Position the vertical 4½in (11.5cm) ruler marks on your ruler along the squared cut that you made in step 3 of Squaring up.

2 With your left hand, press down firmly on the ruler. With your right hand, firmly press down on the rotary cutter and, starting nearest your body, push the cutter away from you through the fabric. Try not to pull the cutter back and forward, as this can cause frayed edges.

3 You can now sub-cut the strip into smaller sections. Line up the ruler over the fabric at the desired width (here we're cutting 4½in/11.5cm squares) and cut as before.

Nesting seams

Place two rows right sides together, and carefully line up the seams. Insert a pin either side of each seam to help keep them perfectly aligned.

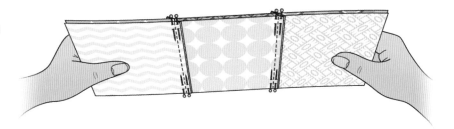

Sewing a nine-square block

These steps show you how to sew a nine-square block. If you are making a larger square block or a rectangular block made up of squares, use the same method to sew the rows and then join them together to complete the block.

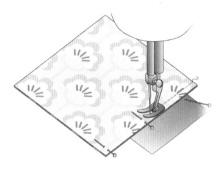

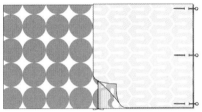

1 Arrange nine squares into three rows of three squares. Move the squares around until you are happy with the arrangement. You can make small numbered paper tags and pin them to each square or row to help you remember the order in which they should be joined.

2 Place the first two squares of the first row together with their right sides facing. Align the raw edges and pin or clip into place. Sew together using a straight machine stitch and a ¼in (0.5cm) seam allowance, removing each pin just before you come to it.

3 Open out the first two squares. Take the third square in the first row and, with the right sides facing, place it onto the right-hand side of the second square. Align the raw edges and pin or clip into place. Sew together in the same way as you did in step 2.

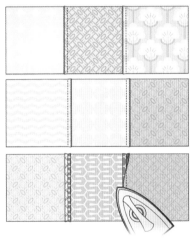

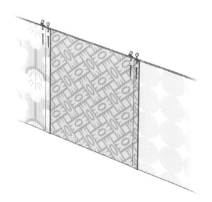

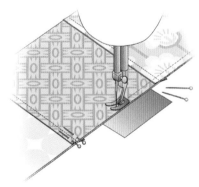

4 Join the second row and then the third row in the same manner. Place the rows in order with their right sides facing down. Press the seam allowances in opposite directions on alternate rows.

5 Place the first two rows together with their right sides facing. Align the raw edges and carefully nest the seams (see page 120). Pin or clip in place.

6 Sew together the two rows, using a straight machine stitch and a ¼in (0.5cm) seam allowance, removing each pin just before you come to it.

7 Open out the first two rows, then join the third row to the second row in the same manner. Press the seams open, or follow the project instructions for which way to press the seams.

Half Square Triangles (HST)

The double method
This method creates two HST at once.

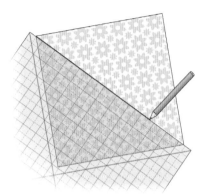

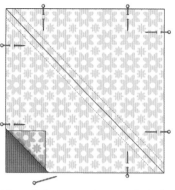

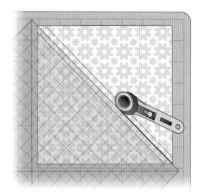

1 Place two squares together with their right sides facing. Using a ruler, draw a diagonal line through the center connecting two corners.

2 Align all the raw edges and pin the squares together. Using a straight machine stitch, sew down each side of the marked line in turn, taking a ¼in (0.5cm) seam allowance from the line.

3 Using a rotary cutter, ruler, and cutting mat, cut along the marked line to create the two HST.

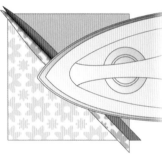

4 On the wrong side of each HST, follow the project instructions to either press the seam allowance open (as shown here) or toward the darker fabric.

5 If you press the seams open, you will need to cut off the little "dog's ears" of fabric that stick out at each end of the seam. If you press the seam toward the darker fabric, there will just be one "dog's ear" to trim off on each side.

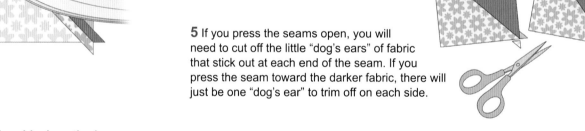

The four-block method
This method creates four HST at once.

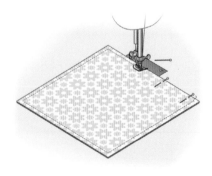

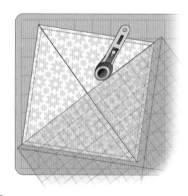

1 Place two squares together with their right sides facing. Pin together. Sew around all four sides of the square using a straight machine stitch and taking a ¼in (0.5cm) seam allowance. Do not leave a gap in the stitching.

2 Using a rotary cutter, ruler, and mat, first place the ruler from corner to corner and cut diagonally through the square. Without separating the cut pieces, rotate the block, place the ruler on the opposite diagonal, and cut through the center of the block a second time.

3 Press open each piece to reveal four Half Square Triangles. Follow steps 4 and 5 of the Double Method to press the seam allowances and cut off the "dog's ears."

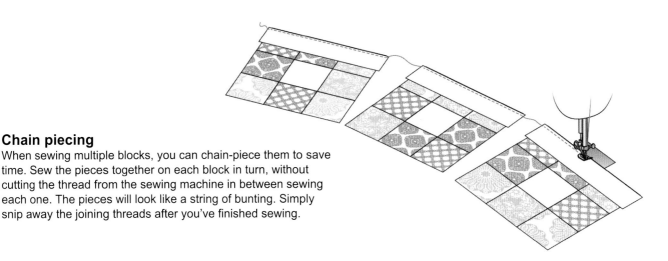

Chain piecing

When sewing multiple blocks, you can chain-piece them to save time. Sew the pieces together on each block in turn, without cutting the thread from the sewing machine in between sewing each one. The pieces will look like a string of bunting. Simply snip away the joining threads after you've finished sewing.

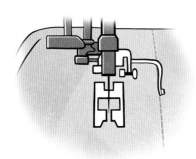

Using a quilting guide bar

A quilting guide bar is a right-angled piece of metal that slides into the back of your sewing machine's foot holder. It's useful when you're sewing straight lines on a finished block or a piece of fabric.

Decide how wide you'd like your quilting lines to be, for example ⅜in (1cm) apart. Using a ruler, set the guide bar ⅜in (1cm) away from the needle. Position the bar on top of the seam line, stitch line, or a drawn guideline. As you stitch, keep the guide bar on the line so your stitching is parallel. If you're sewing lines across the whole piece of fabric, continue sewing the lines using the previous stitch line as your guide, then turn the fabric round and sew the remaining lines.

Attaching binding

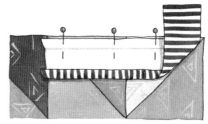

1 With the quilt top right side up, open out the length of binding, align the raw edge with the raw edge of the quilt, and pin in place. When you get to the corner of the first side, fold the binding up away from the quilt. A straight line will be created with the second side of the quilt and the extended binding.

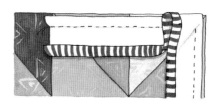

2 Fold the binding back down to align with the next side to be stitched; this will create a small triangle that sits over the corner of the quilt. When you've pinned all sides, overlap the ends of the binding, tucking the raw edges neatly inside, and sew the binding in place, positioning the stitches just inside the crease nearest the raw edge of the binding. Stop sewing just before you come to each small folded triangle, then start sewing again after each triangle.

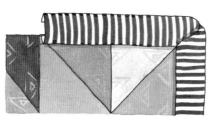

3 Fold the binding over to the back of the quilt, to conceal the raw edges. Neaten the miters over each of the corners and clip or pin in place.

4 Use a needle and thread to hand-sew the binding into place on the back of the quilt using ladder stitch (see page 124).

Hand-sewing and embroidery techniques

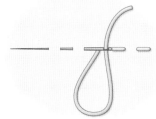

Running stitch
Bring the needle to the surface of the fabric and take it back down to the left of the entry point, to create a straight stitch. Bring the needle back to the surface a stitch length away from the last stitch and return through the fabric as before. Continue to create stitches of equal length.

Basting (tacking) stitch
Basting stitches are used to hold two or more pieces of fabric together temporarily as you work. Using the same method as for running stitch (see above), make long, evenly spaced stitched through the fabric layers. Take several stitches on to your needle at one time, before drawing the thread through the fabric.

Gather stitch
Work a line of running stitches (see above). Pull the needle and the thread gently to gather up the fabric, then secure your stitches.

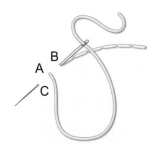

Backstitch
Bring the needle up at A, take it back down one stitch length behind this point at B, and bring it up again at C, one stitch length in front of the point at which it first emerged. Repeat as required.

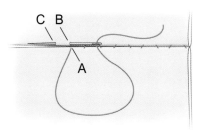

Slipstitch
Slipstitch is nearly invisible and is used to sew up a seam, or a gap in a seam, quickly and easily from the right side of the fabric. Thread the needle and secure the thread. Working from right to left, bring the needle through one folded edge at A, then slip the needle through the fold of the opposite edge at B. Draw the needle and thread through the fabric at C, about ¼in (0.5cm) to the left of B. Continue in this way to join both edges.

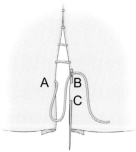

Ladder stitch
This stitch is used to create an invisible seam. Turn in and press the seam allowances. Bring the needle up through the pressed fold at A, then take it straight across the gap to B. Make a tiny stitch through the folded edge and bring it back to the front at C.

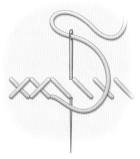

Cross stitch
Work a diagonal stitch, then work back over it to complete the "cross." You can just work a single cross stitch, or a whole line of them.

templates

You can either trace or photocopy the templates that are at 100% (full size). The templates at 50% (half size) will need to be enlarged by 200% on a photocopier.

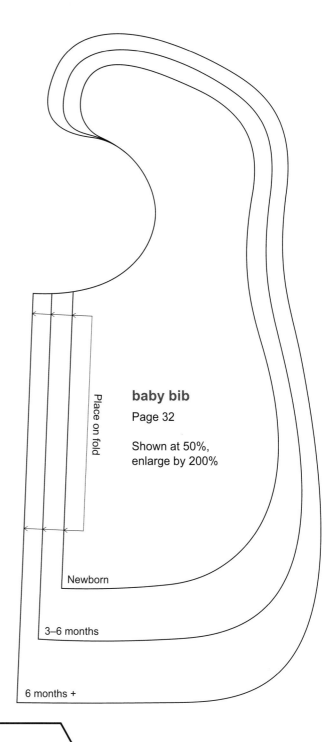

small folded wallet

Page 50

Shown at 50%, enlarge by 200%

baby bib

Page 32

Shown at 50%, enlarge by 200%

Place on fold

Newborn

3–6 months

6 months +

dino taggie lovey

Page 42

Dino appliqué
Shown at 50%, enlarge by 200%

hexi-accent needlebook

Page 26

Paper hexagon
Shown at 100%

hexi-accent needlebook

Page 26

Fussy cutting template
Shown at 100%

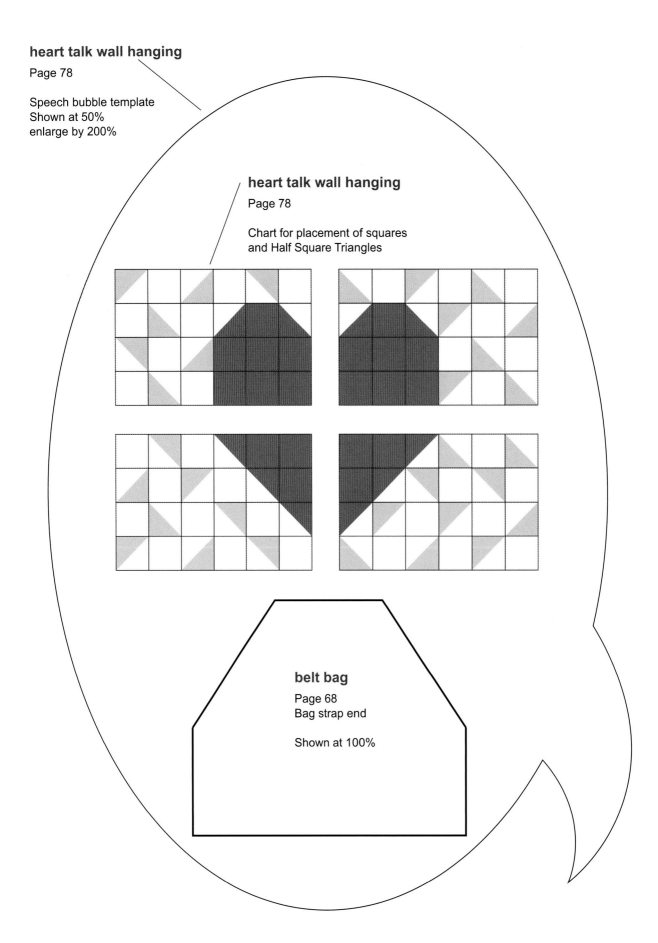

heart talk wall hanging

Page 78

Speech bubble template
Shown at 50%
enlarge by 200%

heart talk wall hanging

Page 78

Chart for placement of squares
and Half Square Triangles

belt bag

Page 68
Bag strap end

Shown at 100%

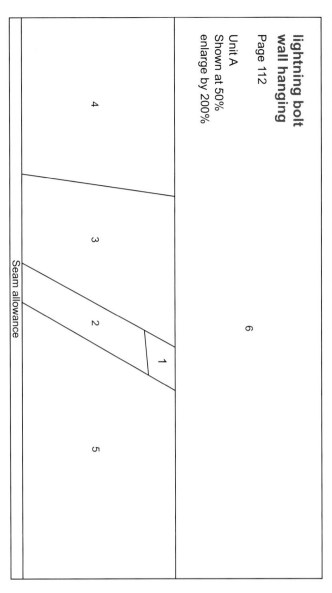

lightning bolt
wall hanging

Page 112

Unit A
Shown at 50%
enlarge by 200%

Seam allowance

4

3

2

1

6

5

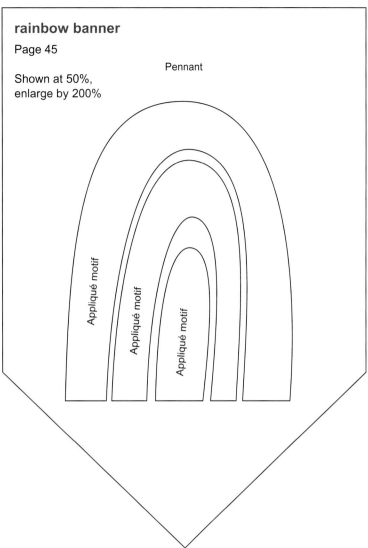

rainbow banner

Page 45

Shown at 50%,
enlarge by 200%

Pennant

Appliqué motif

Appliqué motif

Appliqué motif

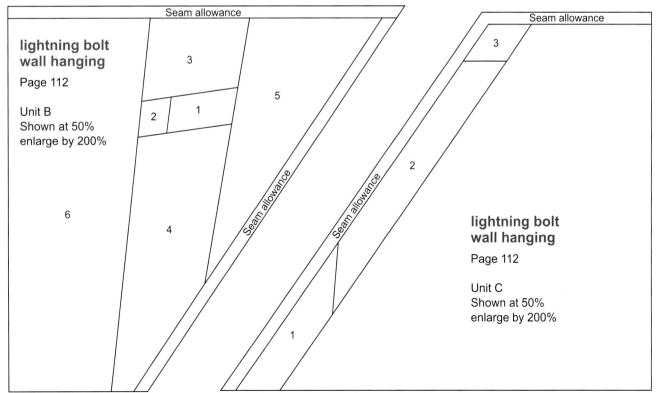

Seam allowance

**lightning bolt
wall hanging**

Page 112

Unit B
Shown at 50%
enlarge by 200%

3

2 1

5

6

4

Seam allowance

Seam allowance

2

1

Seam allowance

3

**lightning bolt
wall hanging**

Page 112

Unit C
Shown at 50%
enlarge by 200%

index

suppliers

UK
Abakhan
www.abakhan.co.uk

Art Gallery Fabrics
www.artgalleryfabrics.com from
UK distributor Hantex Ltd
www.hantexonline.co.uk

Auriful
www.aurifil.com

Cloud9 Fabrics
www.cloud9fabrics.com from
UK distributor Hantex Ltd
www.hantexonline.co.uk

The Fabric Fox
www.thefabricfox.co.uk

Groves
www.grovesltd.co.uk

Hobbycraft
www.hobbycraft.co.uk

John Lewis Haberdashery
www.johnlewis.com

Minerva
www.minerva.com

Oliso
www.oliso.com

Vlieseline
www.vlieseline.com

USA
Andover Fabrics
www.andoverfabrics.com

Art Gallery Fabrics
www.artgalleryfabrics.com

The City Quilter
www.cityquilter.com

Fabric Depot
www.fabricdepot.com

The Fat Quarter Shop
www.fatquartershop.com

Joann
Fabric and craft store
www.joann.com

Michael Miller Fabrics
www.michaelmillerfabrics.com

Michaels
www.michaels.com

acknowledgments

I want to give thanks to all the makers and crafters who have supported my creative journey over the years, many of whom are now cherished and inspiring friends.

Thank you also to the tremendous and talented team at CICO Books. My gratitude goes out to the many people and companies that continue to support my creative work, especially Janet Kolle and Vlieseline. Additionally, I would like to thank the teams at Hantex, Janome, Oliso, and Groves.

Last, but never least, to my husband, John, and our family for the endless support and encouragement.